G~~~~~~~~

TEACHER

WHAT WE LEARN
FROM THE SICK AND DYING

KAREN RUSHEN

Spirituality
& Health
BOOKS

D1056862

Life's Greatest Teacher:
What We Learn from the Sick and Dying

by KAREN RUSHEN
Copyright © 2011 Karen Rushen

Spirituality
&Health BOOKS

425 Boardman Street, Suite C
Traverse City, MI 49684
www.spiritualityhealthbooks.com

Printed in the Canada

Cover and interior design by Barbara Hodge

Cataloging-in-Publication data for this book is available upon request.
ISBN 978-0-9818708-7-8
10 9 8 7 6 5 4 3 2 1

CONTENTS

INTRODUCTION

A SINGLE ENCOUNTER can change the direction of your life. Celine, a thirty-something woman from the slums of Port-au-Prince, was terminally ill with cancer when I found myself assigned to care for her at a home for the dying run by Mother Teresa's sisters in Haiti. Celine responded generously to my nascent caregiving efforts, and that in turn gave birth to a nascent desire in me not only to be useful to the sick and dying, but to learn from them.

As a hospital chaplain, I've found those who are sick and dying to be life's greatest teachers—as can be their sickness and their process of dying. In caring for the sick and the dying, I found myself, time and again, listening in awe to the voice of wisdom. I also benefited from the profound insights shared by many people who have watched their loved ones die. Seared by unfathomable loss, these individuals learned how to rise from the smoking ashes of their ruined lives, not unlike a phoenix, to embrace rich, new lives they would have never hoped for or dreamed of.

All people desire to live generative lives. They want to know that they have put more good than ill into this world and that their unique wisdom, gifts, and life experience have been recognized and valued by those whose lives they've touched. To extend to the sick and dying the kind of compassion that honors them for their hard-earned insights and experience is perhaps one of the greatest comforts we can offer. I have written this book to honor the many sick and dying people whom it has been my privilege to serve, and to tell their stories.

I believe that perhaps *the* greatest comfort we can offer those facing that dark and uncharted terrain we call death is the stories and experiences of those who have traversed that terrain before them. The stories I share in this book help prepare all of us for the inevitable conclusion of our lives. They give us reason to hope that our spirits are not extinguished with our last breath, and they remind us that loving beings await our arrival to a world beyond this one. I have written this book, knowing that my sick and dying patients would want others facing death's terror, pain, and uncertainty to have hope.

PREFACE

FOR THE SAKE OF CONFIDENTIALITY, the stories in this book are composites based on real people's experiences and therefore do not depict specific individuals. I offer you these stories in the hope that you will find them useful on life's great journey. May they help you reflect upon and embrace that which resonates with your own experiences.

Chapter One

A LESSON FROM THE SLUMS OF HAITI

I WAS IN a particularly miserable and fetid slum in Port-au-Prince, where barefoot children in ragged T-shirts ran through rotting garbage heaps where pigs and goats foraged for food. I was there volunteering with Mother Teresa's sisters in their home for the dying as part of an immersion trip to Haiti.

My first "assignment" was Celine, a young Haitian woman dying of cancer. Celine was so slight and curled up so tightly that I could have lifted her off the cot without an effort. Her limbs were dotted with large, hard tumors that looked and felt like wooden tree knobs. The sister in charge of the ward, who looked me up and down uncertainly as if to gauge my potential, or lack thereof, eventually handed me a tin of anesthetic cream, directing me to spend as much time as I could massaging it into Celine's cancerous limbs to relieve her pain.

At first I was so overwhelmed by the situation that I could not move. An American doctor who was working on the ward sensed my distress and asked how he could assist me. Tearfully, I explained that I feared that by massaging this woman, I would only hurt her more, and I told him how frustrated I was that instead of morphine or Vicodin, there was only pain cream on hand. With such an unshakable calm that I wondered if he was sane, the doctor allowed me to vent. And when I finished, he admitted that it was true we lacked adequate medical means to address the situation. Nonetheless, he invited me to put my heart and soul into using the few methods that we did have with "loving intention."

To tell the truth, I was a bit astonished to hear a doctor tell me to do anything with "loving intention," but I got to work on my patient, massaging the cream into every inch of her extremities for the next hour. At first Celine moaned and groaned in protest, yet over time I could sense her relaxing more and even breathing easier. I used "loving intention" as I understood it: I prayed for her. I kept her well-being in the forefront of my thoughts and surrendered my feeble efforts to a power larger than myself—a power that I believed had Celine's ultimate healing and best interests at heart.

The next morning, I went back to the home for the dying and was greeted by a tiny, skeletal Haitian woman perched on one of the windowsills with a sheet wrapped around her bony shoulders and an ear-to-ear grin on her face. She waved at me enthusiastically, patting the sill next to her, inviting me to sit down. I was puzzled. Who was this woman and why was she so adamant to have me join her? Then suddenly I realized that it was Celine, my patient from yesterday. How could she be doing so well? Was the little tin of pain cream actually *that* effective? Astonished, I sat down with my new friend, who took my hand in hers and proceeded to hold it for the next half hour, smiling at me and humming a tune as we enjoyed the sunshine and the cool breeze coming in through the window.

Later I cornered the doctor for an explanation: What had happened here? How was it that one day Celine had been twisted up in pain, and the next she was actually up out of bed and taking a bit of sun, sitting on a windowsill?

The doctor explained that cancer could be like that. Particularly toward the end of their illness, patients could rally and for a while show remarkable energy and interest in life. But he also told me that I should not underestimate the power of the attention—and loving *intention*—that I had given to Celine. Celine had been found abandoned in her own filth, in a gutter in the later stages of terminal cancer, he told me. And now, just one human being taking the time to lavish her with loving care and attention could well have been a powerful enough affirmation of her own dignity and worth to have given her a time of reprieve. This attention may have even afforded Celine a significant degree of peace and inner healing.

I was hooked. From there on, all I wanted to do was take care of more and more sick and dying people. My fears that I might be inadequate were replaced by a sense of wonder and excitement. I could help! I could do something that really mattered to people who found themselves in the worst conceivable circumstances: I could bring them some degree of relief from their physical and emotional pain. And not only that, but when my efforts were inadequate, others would be there to help me. Doctors and nurses would be my friends and allies. The universe itself would kick in to assist me. My prayers would be heard, and my attempts at care and healing would be amplified by powers that were not my own.

It has occurred to me that had I not risked going on that immersion trip to the poorest country in the Western hemisphere, a trip that understandably I'd had many misgivings about, I would never have had such a powerful experience through which to discover so precious a calling as working with the sick and dying. Yet the risk involved went far beyond the chances I took. The sister who ultimately handed me the tin of pain cream took a risk, believing this foreign woman with no medical background would do more good than harm to an already physically and emotionally ravaged patient. As well, the doctor who helped me took significant risks, embracing and passing on to me methods of healing that were far from the conventional beliefs and practices of his trade. My "patient" took a risk surrendering to a foreigner who didn't speak her language for a "medical treatment" whose good, she trusted, might, in the long run, outweigh the initial pain and apparent harm of massaging her cancerous limbs.

Yet, perhaps the biggest risk may have been that this terminally ill woman, who had been "thrown out" by those she had loved and counted on, risked giving her heart yet one more time to one more person when she invited me to join her on that sunny windowsill. Celine's lesson about love hit me like a ton of bricks at a time in my life when I found it increasingly difficult to be a single woman on my own. Celine challenged me to take a chance on love, despite the overwhelming odds and the seeming futility of it all. I realized that if an impoverished and dying woman, abandoned by those she loved, could face life with such courage, love, and generosity of spirit, who was I to nurse my own wounded heart in anger and bitterness?

Taking Risks Determines Whether We Will Live and Die Well

The willingness to risk one's self—to risk taking action in an attempt to find healing for whatever ails us, whether in body, mind, or spirit—and to risk embracing a fuller life is, in my opinion, the single most fundamental thing we will do, or not do, in determining whether we live well and die well. Being willing to take a risk for a better life for ourselves and for others is always the first step in living a "spiritual life"—a life focused not on material gain, but on the invisible matters of the heart, the only "matters" that will really count.

All the great religious traditions have something to teach us about this. Here is a lesson from the Christian tradition, which I believe holds relevance for all peoples:

There was a woman who suffered a hemorrhage for over a dozen years, which essentially means that she never stopped menstruating. At the time of Jesus, menstruation made women ritually unclean and, therefore, subject to all kinds of purity laws that would have kept them alone and isolated from others, particularly men. Touching a man was an especially heinous transgression for a menstruating woman, but this woman risked touching Jesus in an attempt to find healing, because it was her belief that in doing so she could be healed. Thus, this woman broke the law in order to get a better life for herself. And what was Jesus's response to this law-breaking woman? He applauded her and credited her belief and actions for the healing she received.

So many of us, especially women, have been taught to be "good" and that being good means we don't break rules—even bad rules that serve no purpose other than to bolster up the privilege of one group of people over another. We often learn that we are supposed to play it safe in life, so it's best to avoid taking big risks. Yet, ironically, taking risks is where we find a fuller life. Even more ironically, the universe is governed by powers that applaud and support "bad girls" who take risks for the sake of a fuller life. Think about this the next time you find yourself worrying about whether or not to take a risk.

When you work with dying people, you come to understand the importance of risk in light of end-of-life reviews and regrets. All people have regrets, although some have fewer than others for a variety of reasons, and most of the regrets I have heard center on the risks *not* taken. Perhaps it was a particular path one did not choose that may have resulted in a different spouse or career. Or perhaps their regret centered upon a trip or an activity put aside until a future retirement arrived, a retirement that now would not be arriving. I cannot begin to tell you how many hospice patients I have talked to who told me they had "just retired" prior to receiving a terminal diagnosis. Perhaps the most painful regrets I have heard center around a chance at love—or forgiveness—that wasn't taken or was withheld.

Some people deal with issues of staggering proportion and heartbreak, yet come to the end of their lives at peace. Sophie had had three children, the youngest born severely mentally and physically handicapped. On the advice of doctors, Sophie did what was typical seventy years ago: she placed her child in an institution. She spent the rest of her life worrying about that child and wondering if she had done the best thing for her. Yet as Sophie was dying, she came to a remarkable peace about the situation. Partly because of her own experience of physical diminishment and her increasing dependence on others for her personal care, Sophie came to realize that the severity of her child's handicap, as well as the fact that her child had spent her life in an institution, had really been matters out of her control and beyond her ability to handle. She was finally able to forgive herself for doing what, in her mind, she believed no loving mother should have had to do—place her child in an institution. Now Sophie could see that no amount of love would have changed her child's physical and mental condition or enabled her to care for her properly. Yet, this woman was only able to come to this peace of mind at the end of life by taking the risk to examine squarely her greatest fears and regrets instead of insulating herself from those nagging voices inside her head. She was able to see the difference between and make peace with life circumstances that were within her power to change and those beyond her control.

Rhonda, a single mother who had raised four children by herself found out that she was dying of breast cancer just as her last child went off to college, and she was heading off to a long-postponed college education of her own. Rhonda was enraged that she had been left by her husband with inadequate financial means to raise their children and that she was consequently forced to take menial jobs, shelving her life-long desire to be a nurse. Yet when she was able to see that life had left her little choice in terms of her response—she either had to shoulder all the financial and familial responsibilities or, like her husband, walk away—years of anger and resentment melted away. Rhonda realized she had done the best she could, given her circumstances, and a very good job at that. Her children had been her "career," and now she was able to let go of what had been a lifelong dream of going to college with relative peace and ease in the end.

Like many of my patients, Rhonda taught me that ultimately we will not achieve everything we hope for in this life, and, in fact, some of us achieve very few of our dreams. She knew the difference between a life lived for others and a life she might have had pursuing her own hopes and dreams, realizing both were good ways to spend the few years granted her.

What I have found remarkable and sobering is that many of my dying patients have found peace, not so much in terms of which dreams they've achieved, but in reviewing the good they know they've put into the world and the love they've given and experienced, despite the dreams which were never fulfilled.

Both Sophie and Rhonda were able to distinguish between things they could control and things they couldn't. Ultimately, the most painful regret experienced by the dying often seems to be about things they could have changed but chose not to. Those decisions—or lack of decisions—are harder for people to deal with, and a very important and powerful part of working with the dying often involves helping people face, and do something about, those regrets while there's still time.

Mildred, who hadn't talked to her brother in nearly twenty years, wanted no part of him now that she was dying. She made it quite clear to us that we were not to contact her brother, yet she kept telling us that she was having the same dream over and over: she was drawn toward a bright light full of peace, but she was unable to get to the light because there was a big wall in her way.

"What do you think this 'wall' might be?" I asked. And, over time, Mildred acknowledged that she felt it was her angry and unforgiving stance toward her brother. Still, she refused to call him.

Mildred hung on for days—long beyond the point the doctors felt she could have lasted—until her brother finally called her. She accepted the phone call and, shortly after speaking with him, passed on peacefully.

Carmella, an Italian-American woman, had a life-long dream to travel to Sicily to see her mother's village of origin. After being given a terminal prognosis of cancer, she was heartbroken that she would never be able to fulfill her dream. But it was not too late. Drawing up a medical regimen that allowed Carmella to take her dream trip to Italy, the hospice team arranged for her to be accompanied by a cousin who played the role of her own personal nursing assistant on a somewhat more curtailed itinerary than she had initially planned. Upon her return, Carmella spent her remaining days happily entertaining the hospice team with stories of her Italian travels and her experiences in her mother's village.

Every caregiver who has been in the field awhile has his or her own story of a dying patient who officially "ties the knot" with a long-term companion or common-law spouse, often from the confines of a hospital bed with the hospital chaplain officiating. I have witnessed several radiant brides in my career, one even decked out in a wedding gown and veil while hooked to her IV pole. When a caregiver can assist in making such dreams a reality—even in the face of death—it is just as special a gift to the caregiver as it is for patients and their families. It is also a poignant reminder that we do not have unlimited time to fulfill our dreams or to give our loved ones what they need for peace and joy. Still, even when death is imminent, we have it within our means to help others take risks and fulfill dreams, perhaps more so than we can imagine.

Taking Risks in Bite-Size Pieces

When I speak of risk, I'm not talking about foolish or thoughtless behavior with the potential to hurt ourselves or others. The type of risk I am speaking of involves daring to really listen to what's going on inside and to act upon it; being courageous enough to listen, even when what surfaces is pretty ugly.

Are you jealous or envious of someone? It could be that you need to make some changes in your life that would allow you to live more like the person of whom you are jealous. Are you angry about something? Chances are good that you deserve to be. Yet, can you harness that anger for good? Can it be used like rocket fuel to power you toward your goals and dreams, rather than like a lethal weapon that could destroy any further chances of achieving your dreams? Are you simply afraid of taking a risk? Fear is not a bad thing. Frankly, I have a lot of respect for people's fears; we all have fears particular to who we are and what we have experienced. Yet, perhaps your fear is inviting you to ponder taking a particular risk in a manner that, although different from what you have hoped or imagined, will provide you with more comfort and certainty.

There is nothing wrong with taking risks in bite-size pieces. Watching other people die has helped me realize that if I don't act upon my dreams, I'll live a stunted life nagged by envy, anger, and fear. Working with the dying and learning from them has given me the courage and ability to become truly me, even if that means taking risks in bite-size pieces.

When I decided I wanted to work with the sick and dying, I had no career skills which would allow me to assume a paid position in hospice. I had the choice to either do volunteer work or go back for further education in order to fulfill my dream. I wound up choosing both. I did volunteer work to test my "calling." It ran the gamut from sitting with and consoling the terminally ill to cooking their meals and washing their soiled linens. After a couple years of this, I took a leave of absence from my job to do a three-month stint as a chaplain at a hospice. This opportunity came about when the head of human resources read my résumé and asked if I would consider filling in for their chaplain while she was on a leave of absence to have a baby.

I do not possess good math and science skills, so I wasn't suited to be a nurse or doctor. But I do have a background in spirituality and outreach work, and through my volunteer work, I found out that my real skills were best applied in being supportive and "relatively non-judgmental" in critical situations. (I say relatively non-judgmental because I believe learning *not* to judge others is an ideal most of us spend a lifetime perfecting, and I am no exception!) With training, I realized I could become a hospital and hospice chaplain, but the training is often difficult and time-consuming to obtain.

It was at the end of my three months with hospice that something remarkable happened. My parents, who had come into some money because of a few good business investments, gave to me a sum that allowed me to live very simply, but without worry or debt for one year. This enabled me to complete the course requirements I needed to enter the year-long, paid internship toward becoming a hospital and hospice chaplain. I would say this was a remarkable coincidence, but I don't believe in coincidences anymore. More and more, I believe that when we step out in risk, safety nets of all sorts appear beneath our feet and aid us in getting to where it is we need to go.

The Healing Power of Taking Risks

Many of my patients and their families have taken heroic risks in welcoming me as their caregiver and chaplain—risks that have truly humbled me. I have had many Jewish and Muslim patients who have risked trusting that I, a Christian, will not use circumstances to harm or convert them in any manner. I am still in awe whenever an African American family welcomes me—a woman of European heritage—to walk with them during their loved one's illness, often despite their years of negative experience with the dominant white culture. I am equally humbled by the many women who have welcomed me as their chaplain, despite the fact that we were roughly the same age. As someone who has worked with the dying for many years, I can tell you that few things are harder for terminally ill people to deal with than to watch someone of their own age and gender living a vibrant and disease-free life while they themselves are dying; the anger and envy that this stirs up is often more than the patient understandably has the means to deal with. Yet, taking risks of this sort has the power to transform our lives and heal what ails us, physically, spiritually, and emotionally.

When they retired, Lydia and Roger decided to sell everything they had and move overseas to work with the poor in a sprawling slum. Lydia was in remission for breast cancer at the time, so there was no shortage of people to tell this couple how foolishly they were acting. The couple went on to spend fifteen years working among the poor before Roger died of a lingering illness. The people in their community came to the couple's assistance around the clock, offering help, cooking meals, and giving them every sort of physical and emotional care possible. Eventually Lydia, who remained in the country, again despite the advice of many well-meaning people, continued her work after her husband's death and ultimately married one of the doctors who had cared for her husband in his final months.

When we take big risks, especially when we're doing so to bring comfort, healing, and justice to the sick, the poor, and the oppressed of this world, life so very often takes care of us in unexpected ways. It doesn't mean our lives will be lived unscathed by pain and sadness, but it does mean that we will often be provided with the strength, means, and aid to get where we need to go.

One of my most memorable teachers was Helen, a woman in her mid-seventies who was dying of cancer when I met her. After being single most of her life, Helen married a widower in her mid-fifties, acquiring doting step-children and step-grandchildren. She had a successful career exhibiting and selling her oil paintings and traveling all over the world with her husband.

Whenever I went to visit Helen, she would show me all her souvenirs from her many overseas trips. Eventually, I had to come to terms with the fact that I was jealous of her, and when we were at a point when making the admission to Helen would do her good, I risked telling her. Sometimes, admitting to others that we have a healthy envy of their good fortune can help them appreciate even more the gift that their particular life's path has been. Yet, my envy of Helen proved to be a gift to me as well. It allowed me to see what risks I needed to take in my own life in order to find someone to marry and to make time to fulfill my own dreams.

In sharing my envy with Helen, I allowed her to give me a very precious gift: the assurance that I would be in her prayers so that I might discover and pursue those things that would, in my own dying moments, give me a sense of having lived a rich, full, and deeply meaningful life. The risk I took in sharing my envy with her also wound up being a gift to her. It provided Helen with the opportunity to give something to someone—her prayers and her best wishes—even as she was dying, which made her feel important, special, and still generative.

The fact that we are all going to die—some sooner than others—is really an unwelcome gift of sorts, because it reminds us that we do not have unlimited time to follow our hearts and dreams; and our hearts and dreams will not be silenced, even as we lay dying. The first step on any spiritual journey is risk: risking to trust your own inner voice, risking to trust what life presents to you, and then further trusting that life's resources—both human and divine—will be sufficient for whatever tasks present themselves. Embracing and undertaking the spiritual journey is the first step to a full, rich, and meaningful life—a life that, when death is imminent, will give us deep comfort, support, and peace. Having lived such a life will allow us to be able to let go just a little bit easier and to risk the next step in the journey that awaits us.

Chapter Two

COMPANIONS FOR THE JOURNEY

Miss Hurley was dying, and all she could think about was Nibbles. An elderly hospice patient with few friends and no family, Miss Hurley loved her cat, Nibbles, and had received significant emotional support from her feline friend throughout her decline. Complications at the end of her life had landed her in our hospital's inpatient palliative care unit where it appeared Miss Hurley was destined to spend her final days without Nibbles. Due to the hospital's policy that no animals of any kind were allowed inside the building, presumably for health reasons, the nurses watched helplessly as Miss Hurley repeatedly inquired after her friend and then wept at Nibbles's absence, all as she lay dying. Eventually, our nurses did what so many nurses do best when faced with difficult situations with no easy answers: they broke the rules in favor of their patient's well-being. One of the nurses secured Miss Hurley's house keys from the hospice team, drove over to her home, put Nibbles in her kitty carrier, and brought her back to Miss Hurley's room. Upon seeing Nibbles, Miss Hurley wept tears of joy and, with her cat snuggled in bed next to her, peacefully drifted off into a sleep from which she never awoke.

All of us need companions on this journey we know as life, whether those companions be friends, family, caring professionals, or simply those special "creature companions." In the dying process, the need for companionship becomes especially important and poignant. The dying come to recognize that they are unable to care for themselves and that they therefore need help with more and more of life's daily tasks. They also have a need to give others something of themselves—to feel that their own lives are and were generative and worthwhile. Very often they need aides to reconcile the injustices and difficulties they've faced. "Go-betweens" can help them reconcile with loved ones. And they often desperately seek the company and wisdom of those who have witnessed the dying process; professionals and companions who have looked into the face of death time and again can help the dying navigate that lonely and often terrifying journey.

Our Need for Different Companions at Different Stages of Dying

Years ago I had a patient from Nigeria who had been diagnosed in the advanced stages of terminal cancer while she was in the States visiting her daughter. Since sending her back to Africa was really not an option, given her advanced state of illness, Rose was admitted to our hospital to have her symptoms stabilized before being released to our home hospice program. However, Rose's daughter refused to have her mother returned to her home under the care of our hospice personnel. Sometimes, the daughter claimed, she was overwhelmed with other duties and therefore unable to care for her mother. At other times, she simply told us she was terrified of having a dying person under the same roof. To be fair, Rose's daughter was only in her mid-twenties—a point in life when many young people might feel that caring for a dying parent is way beyond their resources. Because Rose lacked health insurance and was, as a foreign visitor to our country, ineligible for either Medicare or Medicaid, finding another facility or nursing home for her final weeks of care was next to impossible. So Rose stayed at our hospital and became part of our family.

At first this arrangement appeared to be working. Rose was as delightful, generous, and upbeat as one can be while dying of cancer, and the entire staff loved her. At Rose's request, I would visit daily, and during our visits Rose would hold my hand, offering a virtual litany of praise and thanksgiving for the compassionate and skilled care our medical team was giving her.

As time passed and Rose's condition worsened, she became more and more depressed and withdrawn from the staff. Predictably enough, the idea of dying in a foreign country, surrounded by foreigners, was too much for her. Initially our care and affection had met many of Rose's needs, but as she grew closer to death her need to experience the norms of her African society grew acute. In her culture, it is the family who cares for the dying; she needed to know she was loved by her family by being cared for by them physically in her final days. Demanding that she be taken home, Rose pressed the medical team to intervene and force her daughter to take her in. Even more than physical care, Rose needed to reconcile her sense of self-worth and her relationship with her daughter.

Of course, no one could force Rose's daughter to take her in, nor would it have been a very good scenario were we able to do so. Instead, the medical team called several conferences with the family to bring about some healing between mother and daughter and to assure the daughter that, in taking her mother into her home, she would not be overwhelmed or left alone. She would have the care and wisdom of the hospice team at her service twenty-four hours a day for as long as she needed them.

Eventually, buoyed with a new sense of pride and inner peace, Rose left our hospital to spend her final days with her daughter. Her daughter, imbued with a new sense of confidence in her ability to care for her mother, and with a sense of pride and purpose, was now able to embrace the responsibility of caring for her mother in her final days, as was African tradition.

Lois—My Very Own "Morrie"

I have always loved Mitch Albom's book *Tuesdays with Morrie*, about his relationship and final conversations with his dying professor, Morrie Schwartz. I remember when the book first came out how many people thought Morrie Schwartz was a remarkable and unusual man in his desire to share the dying process with others. While I have no argument about Morrie Schwartz having been a remarkable man, I would like to suggest that he isn't that "unusual." There are many, many "Morries" out there—dying men and women eager to share with others what living has taught them. To one degree or another, each of my patients has acted as my very own "Morrie," but perhaps the patient who wound up being one of my most intentional teachers was an elderly Jewish widow who, when she found out I was a chaplain-in-training, took me under her wing so that she could help me as much as, if not more than, I could help her.

The first time I met Lois, she was sitting by the huge living room window of her condominium with its breathtaking view of Chicago's most extensive park and Lake Michigan. She was crocheting frantically. Lois explained to me that she had five grandchildren, each of whom she wanted to leave a "treasured memento," and that she was only on "afghan number three" with what now appeared to be limited time ahead of her. Would I mind much if she knitted or crocheted while we had our visits?

Next to Lois, stacked two feet high off the floor, was a collection of all kinds of books on death and dying. She explained that she was doing "research." Would I mind very much if some of our visiting time could be spent reviewing the things Lois was learning about the dying process?

I had no objections; in fact, I found Lois and her art-filled condominium and inquisitive nature, as well as her generous and generative disposition, simply fascinating. I was a brand new chaplain-in-training, and Lois seemed to me to be the kind of older woman I hoped to become—big-hearted, good-humored, artistically prolific, witty, open to learning, and, above all else, deeply loving.

Still, Lois was also quite understandably afraid of dying. She wasn't certain she had anything to "look forward to after dying," as she put it, and her lung cancer prognosis made it as difficult and frightening a way to die as either of us could imagine. So Lois and I made a contract: I would be with her till the end, promising to come and simply sit with her on a regular basis even when it appeared that Lois was long beyond the point of recognizing, needing, or responding to me. Lois, in turn, promised to "teach" me how to be the good chaplain I was hoping to become. This meant that Lois would evaluate all my visits, telling me precisely what was—or wasn't!—helpful to her. This might sound a tad intimidating except that Lois was so kind, gentle, and specific in her observations—including gems like remembering to pop a breath mint in my mouth before a visit after a cup of coffee, because so many cancer patients are so sensitive to smell; or remembering something as simple as offering people the option of a hand to hold as I spoke with them. To this day, I practice much of what Lois taught me.

Lois gave me yet another very special gift. During one of my visits, she told me about a book she was reading that was describing out-of-body experiences, and she wanted to know if I believed in them. I explained that I had never had an out-of-body experience, but that already, in my nascent chaplaincy career, I was hearing stories from nurses and other chaplains about patients claiming to "leave their body" and "travel" to see old friends, family, and places from their youth, although a common observation was that their loved ones could not see or hear them. The possibility of being able to leave her failing body, if her breathing were to become too difficult, gave Lois a lot of comfort. She promised me that if she were ever able to do so, she'd visit me and let me know. I reminded Lois that other patients had expressed sadness over the inability to communicate their presence, but Lois just laughed and told me not to worry; she'd find a way to make her presence known. We laughed about this, and then I promptly forgot about it—that is, until Lois dropped by one morning for a visit.

Soon after our conversation, Lois began to decline rapidly. I kept my promise and made my vigils at her bedside, holding her hand and sitting quietly with her, although Lois was unresponsive for the most part. It was during this time that a friend and I went up the west coast of Michigan for a long weekend getaway at a bed and breakfast. In the morning, I awoke with the distinct and eerie feeling that someone other than my friend was in the room with me. The "presence" I felt was palpable, and while somewhat unnerving, it seemed not only "friendly" but also positively effusive and joyful to an extent that both baffled and fascinated me. It was one of the most unusual and remarkable experiences of "another" that I ever had. Ultimately, the "presence" simply drifted off and left me wondering, "Could that have been Lois?" Almost as if in response to my query, I felt goose bumps run up and down my arms.

When I got back to work, I immediately went to visit Lois. She was still alive. Though she was unresponsive, I told her about my experience. "I bet that was you, wasn't it, Lois, trying to show me that out-of-body experiences do exist and are possible, right?" I said almost teasingly, whereupon Lois, who had been unresponsive for nearly three weeks, squeezed my hand and smiled! I nearly had a heart attack.

Now, when patients ask me about out-of-body experiences or the possibility of an existence beyond this one, I tell them about Lois and the unique gift she gave to me. I am certain that Lois would be pleased that so much of what she taught me gave hope and comfort to so many other dying patients and their families, and that she would be satisfied in knowing, even while dying, that she was able to leave behind a "treasured memento" of her time here on Earth.

Companions in Our Final Days on Earth

Some patients do not possess the generosity of spirit that Lois had, nor do they express the same need for companionship. Sometimes, life has been so hard for them that they arrive at its end too battered and bruised to be able to reach out to anyone. They have carefully hidden a need for companionship, almost without being conscious of it, because of repeated sufferings in the past. And yet, time and again, I have seen these stricken people receive what they need at the end of life so that they are able to heal some of their deep wounds and face their deaths with a sense of peace.

My husband, Stephen, who is originally from Ireland, is also a chaplain. Every time there is an Irish patient in the hospital (and there are always more than you'd expect!), he is called to their bedside. One of Stephen's patients was an elderly bachelor named Denny who came to the United States nearly half a century ago from an impoverished village in western Ireland, seeking and finding work in the construction industry. Injured on the job and never able to earn as much as he hoped, Denny became withdrawn and fell into a depression. He sustained few significant relationships during his time in the States and had become estranged from his family back in Ireland.

In his final days, Denny's companionship with Stephen proved to be quite healing. As the two got talking about the "old country," Stephen managed to convince Denny to contact his family. Denny's parents and siblings had long since died, but he had nieces and nephews who were grateful to reconnect with their long-lost uncle. After Denny passed away, Stephen, who was scheduled for a visit back to Ireland anyway, volunteered to carry Denny's ashes home and deliver them to one of the nieces at the airport. Over a full Irish breakfast and a glass of stout, Stephen and Denny's niece were able to offer a toast to this patient's long and often difficult life, as well as welcome him back to the country of his birth, into the arms of a family waiting to reunite with him, to finally be put to rest beside family members.

Ultimately each of us dies alone and in our own unique way; no one else can die with us or for us. As people get nearer and nearer to death, they seem to begin to withdraw, scaling back emotional availability from a large cadre of supportive medical staff, friends, and family to only a tiny contingent of loved ones. In their final days, I have seen many, many patients turn most of their limited energies toward what appears to be a new set of "companions"— those who appear to await them in the next life. This new set of companions helps them in the dying process. They are often loved ones who have already passed on, or they are important religious or spiritual figures whom the dying person claims to see and with whom they have communicated.

I remember one particular patient, Tom, who entered our inpatient hospice unit in a horrendous state, terrified of dying and in awful pain. The hospice team was able to address his physical pain fairly quickly and efficiently, but no one seemed able to alleviate Tom's "inner pain"—his terror of dying.

I was called in to pray with him, and I must admit Tom's terror was so absolute that, despite my best intentions and my prayers, I felt completely ill-equipped to help him. I left his side feeling certain I had done nothing for him. Yet it is important for us as caregivers to remember two things. First, we are caregivers, not miracle workers, and we can only give and do our best. Second, our patients—sometimes despite us rather than because of us—often get the "miracle" they need precisely when they need it.

Soon after I had prayed with Tom, one of the nurses came to tell me of something profound that she had witnessed. Stepping into the Tom's room, she saw him transfixed, staring straight ahead, his terror gone, with a look of joy and wonder. He turned to the nurse and asked if she, too, saw the beautiful woman standing in front of him. Of course, the nurse saw no one—no one else was in the room—but instead of contradicting the patient, she asked him what the beautiful woman wanted. Tom said she had come to tell him he was going to be all right, and that within twenty-four hours she would return to take him home with her. All the nurses on the unit looked at their watches and were not surprised when on the next day—twenty-three hours and fifty minutes later—the man passed away very peacefully.

Working with the sick and dying has taught me that not only do all of us need companionship at all stages of life, but that at particular stages we need particular types of companions to provide us with a kind of companionship and accompaniment that even our dearest loved ones may not be able to offer. Those of us who are left behind after the death of a loved one need companions in our journey through grief; they are friends who are gentle and sympathetic to the course that sorrow runs, and companions who can assist us in finding new life after the death of a loved one when such "new life" seems nearly impossible to find.

I remember Olivia's mother. Olivia was born with a multitude of serious problems and birth defects, and she spent her entire life—a mere three months—in the Neonatal Intensive Care Unit. Olivia's mother was devastated when her daughter died and came to bereavement support counseling for months, showing little sign of healing from the pain of the loss of her daughter. In truth, Olivia's mother seemed more and more distraught as the months passed.

One day, about nine months after Olivia's death, Olivia's mother had a breakthrough as she sat crying, holding the little, handmade quilt that had served to keep Olivia's tiny body warm while she struggled for life in our Neonatal ICU. Olivia's mother treasured the quilt; not only had it comforted her child, but Olivia's mother had held and rocked her little daughter wrapped in that quilt as she died. It symbolized a link. She was profoundly grateful for it, yet she realized that she had no idea where this quilt had come from, although obviously it was carefully and lovingly made by hand.

Olivia's mother inquired as to the quilt's origins at our next bereavement counseling session, and I was able to find out that it had been made and donated to the hospital by a woman who also had lost a child. This woman had made it her personal mission to sew quilts for other people's babies, praying for the quilts' tiny recipients and their loved ones while she stitched. Olivia's mother was so touched by someone who had turned her own sadness and loss into a ministry of outreach that she also began making baby quilts for other families dealing with a dying child. Eventually, Olivia's mother became quite an advocate for parents who had suffered from the death of a child, and she spent countless hours giving them the type of comfort and support she'd garnered from her painful firsthand experience.

I was at a women's interfaith conference where I met Itedal, a lovely Palestinian-American, who was proud of her heritage and wore the *hijab,* the traditional head covering worn by Muslim women. We hit it off immediately and, as we got to know one another better, we began talking about our careers. When Itedal found out I was a chaplain-in-training at the local hospital, she was initially at a loss for words. "You have been brought into my life for a purpose," she finally said, and she proceeded to explain that three years ago her young husband had been brought into our ER after being involved in an automobile accident, and he subsequently died here from injuries. On one hand, she was profoundly grateful for the wonderful care she and her husband had received from the staff, extolling the ER chaplain who walked with her through that horrible day with care and tenderness in a manner that was respectful of her Muslim beliefs. On the other hand, she regretted that, on the very worst day of her life and at the precise moment she could have used the spiritual guidance of an imam, there was no such Muslim chaplain on duty.

"The area just west of your hospital has a burgeoning Muslim population," she explained. "In fact, in the town where I live over thirty percent of the people are Muslims. In honor of my husband's memory, I have found myself wanting to speak with medical workers to explain to them how they could best deal with their Muslim patients. I also have a dream that no Muslim family in our community will ever go through what I went through without the assistance of a Muslim chaplain."

Itedal's efforts and insights were instrumental in assisting the hospital in becoming the first in our metropolitan area to train and hire a Muslim chaplain.

Companions for Our Spiritual Journey

We who hope to be spiritual companions to the sick and dying likewise need companions on our own spiritual journeys. How and where do we find them? Sometimes, these companions, like life's lessons, find us.

One of the doctors on our hospice medical team seemed especially wary and critical of me. This stung my pride as well as my heart because Dr. Anne was the type of person I really admire—capable and competent, with a gentle, but direct, bedside manner, passionate and tireless in regard to her patients and their well-being. Certainly I was striving to be all these things. So, I wondered, why didn't Dr. Anne like me?

One day after Dr. Anne, a hospice nurse, and I returned from seeing a patient and family for a consult in their home, the doctor expressed to me that I had done a particularly good job dealing with the family and the issue at hand. Heartened by this compliment, I decided to take a risk: I mentioned that I didn't always get the feeling that she liked or approved of my bedside manner. Dr. Anne made a face and hesitated, but she did admit that there were things I was saying and doing that were of concern to her. For example, she had heard me speaking about a past patient who was "cured" of her cancer. (A patient had come into our hospice program with cancer, and was later discharged without any apparent reason, with the cancer having—at least in my book—been "cured.") Dr. Anne was concerned when she heard me speaking about this; she wanted me to understand that no one is "cured" of cancer. The truth is that cancer can go into remission, sometimes for years, and in some cases even for the rest of the patient's natural life.

Evidently, Dr. Anne was concerned that, as the team's chaplain, I might be "one of those chaplains" who gives patients and families false hope about an imminent miracle. I was a little miffed—especially at being called "one of those chaplains." But overall, I could "hear" that not only was Dr. Anne's heart in the right place, but she was correct in suggesting that if I were going to be an effective member of the medical team as well as a good chaplain, I needed to learn medical and scientific facts. I needed to be aware of how cancer works, and to be able to speak in a doctor's language. And I needed to be able to address patients and their desire for a miracle cure in a manner that wouldn't mislead them or give them false hope.

After our open and honest airing of mutual concerns, Dr. Anne and I actually became very good friends. She became a mentor, and my relationship with her has lasted many years beyond my work with that particular medical team and hospital and into other positions at other facilities.

Sometimes, the spiritual companion we are seeking is right under our nose, but we don't see him. During my residency year as a chaplain-in-training, I was in a class with four other residents learning to be hospital chaplains. One of them was a very kind, quiet man of few words. We often worked together, particularly in the ER and on some of my toughest cases involving infant deaths, or the sudden and unexpected deaths of brain-injured individuals. Gradually, I began to notice that whenever I had a tough case, he always volunteered to accompany me. I was happy about this, because his gentle demeanor immediately put our patients and their families at ease, and there was little he wouldn't do for them.

Over time, I came to like and admire him, but it never occurred to me that he might like and admire me back, or that one day, he might turn out to be a wonderful life partner. At the time, I was too busy juggling two other guys: a businessman who, while taking me out to expensive restaurants, was almost as unavailable as the doctor I was also dating, who seemed to love my attention, but who gave me way too little of his own. While I was running around trying to figure out how to "make things work," I hardly gave a second thought to steady, dependable, and quiet Stephen. It took one of the other chaplains to point out to me that when anything happened around the department that involved me, Stephen became interested, available, helpful, and doggedly present to the end. As you might have suspected, I wound up marrying him. Sometimes life's gift of a companion has to hit us over the head.

Working in a hospital environment can be taxing, and over the years I have come to appreciate the wisdom of self-care. For me, self-care includes lots of "crafting," because, like Olivia's mother who found healing in making baby quilts, I find tremendous healing and renewal of spirit in creating something beautiful. At one of the hospitals, I could see that our medical staff had a profound need for opportunities that could renew their own spirits, so I formed a small craft group, inviting staff to come and relax while making dolls to give to impoverished children, greeting cards for women in domestic violence shelters, and beaded jewelry for troubled teens. Our crafts group not only did a lot of good for the community, but it also did our group a lot of good by generating new friendships as we shared each other's company.

Sewing dollies and assembling beaded bracelets are not "sexy"—they won't cure cancer, end world hunger, or solve issues of racism. But the dying have taught me that every little thing we do—indeed precisely the little things we do—count in ways that we are not able to fathom or appreciate from the perspective of this life. We are not all asked to cure cancer, and each of us can do our small part toward ending world hunger and racism. What we are really asked to do is to examine our respective lives, including our individual dispositions and talents, and then make our individual and unique contribution to the well-being of others and this planet.

The Right Companion at the Right Moment

Some companions walk with us for years, while others only walk with us for hours. Yet the brevity of some spiritual companionship does not mean it is insignificant. I once reviewed my on-call cases for a semester and discovered that, on average, I spent around an hour and twenty minutes on each case, sometimes much less and, of course, sometimes much, much more. Not a lot of time, yet for the sick and the dying I visited, it was time of disproportionate importance to its duration.

My husband and I were shopping at one of those big box stores one evening, when a young woman in tears approached Stephen. My husband had been the chaplain on duty when her father died two years before, and she thanked him so profusely and with such emotion that I had to excuse myself to step away to fight back my tears.

Another time, I was at a social gathering where I was approached by an older African American woman who grabbed my hand warmly and announced to everyone assembled there that, "This is the woman who was with me at the hospital the night my husband was murdered." You can imagine how that announcement changed the tone of our gathering!

Remember Olivia's mother, the woman whose grief led her to a ministry of making crib quilts for families of sick and terminally ill infants? I met Olivia's mother and father while making rounds on the Neonatal ICU in the last three hours of Olivia's life. I had never met this couple before, yet there I was, the chaplain who was going to accompany them through the most horrible and tragic moments of their lives—the death of their beloved only child. As a chaplain, I find myself in these "worst moments" again and again and again. Yet, it has been one of the greatest blessings of my life to be able to be there and to be able to offer to others my presence, my prayers, and my experience.

Remember Miss Hurley and her cat, Nibbles? This story has a thought-provoking ending. The minute Miss Hurley died—and our medical team had a fairly precise idea of when that was, at least in terms of organ functions—Nibbles, who hadn't moved an inch prior to her passing, hopped off the bed and headed down the hall, where a nurse intercepted him on her way into the room from the nursing station. I guess once Miss Hurley had died, Nibbles was officially "off duty."

What's the lesson to be learned here? Is it that life moves on cruelly without us after our passing? I don't think so. The dead must go their way, and we must go ours. That is the reality of loving relationships on this plane of existence. We who remain here will always know and feel the love of those who have moved on, but we must search for life—for other companions—till the time of our own passing. This doesn't mean that the dead simply forget us, or we them. We simply must keep going in order to care for ourselves—in body, mind, and spirit—because it is imperative to our continuing journey.

Chapter Three

OBEY THE BODY

WHEN I BEGAN MY TRAINING as a chaplain in a large, urban trauma center, a lot of my friends asked if being on staff was anything like ER, the televised medical drama du jour of my era. I answered somewhat predictably: "Well yes, some of the time it is." What about all that sexual tension on medical dramas, complete with medical staff falling into bed with one another on a regular basis? Well, some of the time, yes, you do encounter that. How about all the violence and horror, with shootouts in the ER, and screaming, dysfunctional patients and families? I wish that kind of misfortune and violence were just Hollywood inventions, but actually yes to that too. These things happen, although not on a weekly basis, thankfully. How about all the bizarre injuries? Yes, definitely yes to that one too; people get injured or die in ways that, before my chaplaincy years, I would have found hard to imagine. And what about all those addictions one sees—to power and performance as well as drugs and alcohol . . . and brownies? OK, so those medical soap operas don't often focus on all the goodies at the nursing stations, but yes, yes, and yes to addictions running rampant in any given medical setting, especially to junk food at the nursing station, which we will address later in this chapter.

I have worked in hospitals where staff have killed coworkers or themselves while on duty, where there were shootings and gang fights in the ER, where a patient was shot and killed by her husband as she lay in her hospital bed and then he turned the gun on himself, and where patients have run through plate glass windows or leapt off the roof of the hospital, falling to their deaths. I will not bore or titillate you with the bizarre nature of injuries caused by a staggering and unlikely collection of household objects that come into emergencies rooms, many of them involving questionable sexual practices. Nor will I expound upon the inappropriate places where staff find patients trying to have sex. (The joke, of course, is that staff are usually more discreet because they know all the best hiding places; I have worked in several hospitals where it actually had to be stated that having sex on the job was grounds for dismissal.) And then, of course, we had patients and their loved ones trying to injure or kill one another—when they thought staff weren't looking, that is!

Yet, despite all this violence, death, dysfunction, and destruction—or perhaps because of it!—there is something about being in a hospital, about working with the sick and dying and being so close to so much death, that usually makes us want to live . . . and live with a vengeance. Consequently, when we are faced with such a strong urge to live in the face of so much death, all the body's physical needs and urges suddenly stand up and demand our attention with an urgency that is simply staggering. And what do those physical needs and urges look like? Just think of the bottom four tiers of Maslow's hierarchy of needs: sex, food, intimacy, and rest.

Most of us reading this book are fortunate enough to occupy a place in the top tier of Maslow's hierarchy of needs: personal achievement, getting respect from others, living creative and fulfilled lives, and becoming self-actualized. We are, after all, the readers of self-help books! Yet often today, we find ourselves trying to fulfill these needs at the expense of caring for our most basic ones—proper rest, recreation, nourishment, and intimacy. As caregivers working with the sick and dying, we cannot afford to ignore or shortchange what's basic. If we ignore these needs, sooner or later we are going to crash and burn, rendering ourselves useless to others as well as ourselves. A caregiver quickly learns one thing: obey the body or suffer the consequences—consequences which could literally be deadly.

Balance Versus the Biscuits and Gravy Diet

When I began training as a chaplain, I had my own plan of care to address those bottom-tier needs which made themselves acutely known to me after my eighteen- and twenty-four-hour shifts. Once or twice a week, I had an on-call shift that began at two p.m. and ended at eight thirty a.m. the next day. If I was working an occasional weekend shift, I was on duty twenty-four hours straight (from eight thirty a.m. to eight thirty the following morning). We chaplains had an on-call room where we were actually allowed to sleep during our shifts, in the event that patients didn't need our services. This meant that I was usually in bed about eleven p.m., if I was lucky. Lots of patients become lonely and afraid at night, and it wasn't uncommon for me to get paged late in the evening to "say a prayer with" a patient, often a ruse to coax the chaplain to come and sit with them.

I was usually called several times during the night. My pager would buzz me out of a dead sleep, and I would be out of bed and on my way down the hall with an astonishing amount of clarity and energy that I attribute to a mix of adrenaline and grace. While most of the city slept, I was present at codes, consoling the family members of a patient who had just died in the ER from a traffic accident or gunshot wound, or in one of our intensive care units where a patient had most likely coded.

When everything was over and the family members had departed from the hospital, it was often two or three a.m., and I was still wide awake. So I would wander down to our hospital's twenty-four-hour coffee shop, where I would sit with a warm drink, preferably without caffeine, staring out the black-glass windows beyond my distorted reflection into the dark night of the city. There I pondered the sufferings and the mysteries of this life that had just stared me in the face, until drowsiness began tugging me back to bed . . . until the next time the pager went off.

After I left the hospital at eight thirty the next morning, I would head to a wonderful little greasy spoon in a leafy neighborhood of quiet streets and old bungalows near my home. I would find a cozy booth by the window and watch the day unfold, indulging in a hearty breakfast of eggs over easy with ham or sausage patties and a side of biscuits and gravy or potato pancakes. Never mind that I was a vegetarian! I was famished after walking ten miles or more per shift.

Accompanied by a tall glass of fresh-squeezed orange juice and an endless cup of decaf coffee, this comfort-food breakfast produced just the right chemical reaction in me, for the minute I stepped into the house, I would fall into bed and sleep soundly for hours. Usually I'd wake up around mid-afternoon, take an hour-long walk around the neighborhood, head home to do yoga, cook myself a vegetarian meal, and finally spend the evening in some restorative activity— either reading, visiting with friends, or "vegging out" in front of the television. Following such a regimen, I'd be ready for bed around ten p.m., able to get back on a relatively normal pattern of sleeping, at least until my next overnight shift.

Now, before you dismiss me as some sort of nut for my "healing regimen" of breakfast sausage, potato pancakes, and TV viewing, or run off to tell your friends that you've finally found the self-help solution of your dreams, let me say one thing: It's all about balance. I am not going to argue the dietary pros and cons of fried sausage patties and potato pancakes; obviously, this isn't the best food for you on a regular basis. Still, I would argue that taken in moderation, especially when balanced with a largely vegetarian diet and plenty of rest and exercise, an occasional indulgence in breakfast sausage and potato pancakes probably won't kill you. Neither will a small dose of mindless television. The problem plaguing so many of us is that we are out of balance so much of the time.

My contingent chaplain's self-care regimen of a hearty breakfast balanced with a vegetarian meal, a midday nap, a little bit of exercise, and some enjoyable down time was an imperfect attempt at best to putting a disrupted life back in order. Without a doubt, the preferred modus operandi of any caregiver would consist of an eight-hour work day, adequate sleep, a healthy diet full of fruits, vegetables, and fiber, plenty of good liquids, exercise, recreation, intimacy, and spiritual practice, all "practiced" in a safe, clean, and healthy environment free of stress, filth, and chaos. However, as we all know, this perfect world has yet to be established permanently on this plane of existence. So we must continue striving to do the best we can, and when life gets out of balance, we need to re-center ourselves, beginning again as often as needed.

Our health-care system, not to mention our world, is out of balance, so we who are caregivers have to operate in a world out of balance. It is in part why some medical staff are "killing themselves," either with prescription drugs, guns, or food. It is also why we see so much violence and dysfunctional relationships and behaviors in hospitals. So many people have lost their balance, living lives which ultimately push them beyond the breaking point.

Facing life and caring for others in an unbalanced world is demanding. We must care for ourselves, aggressively and thoroughly, or we will not be able to help ourselves, let alone others. My little regimen of self-care met most of my immediate needs—and "immediate" is the operative word for a mind and body that have been overtaxed and even traumatized on shift in a trauma center. My regimen replenished a weary self with food, rest, sleep, even intimacy to some degree, as I became well acquainted with the staff at the diner. It also allowed me "alone time," a kind of intimacy that many of us neglect to foster. Spending alone time sleeping, eating, and exercising also helped me to be intimately available to friends and loved ones in the long run. Yet ultimately, my regimen was just that—mine. Perhaps one of the single most helpful things caregivers can do for themselves is devise and follow their own personalized healing regimen, comprised of healthy practices and recreational activities that have the capacity to restore body, mind, and spirit.

Creating a Healing Regimen

When we are living or working in an extremely stressful, taxing, or debilitating situation, equally extreme measures of self-care may be needed to bring balance back into our lives. I would argue that in order to care for others, we must care for ourselves first, lovingly and indulgently. And caring for ourselves means knowing when we are particularly debilitated, and then treating ourselves to a corresponding degree of self-care. To borrow some medical terminology, we who are caregivers need to learn how to "triage"—meaning to first honor and address our own most urgent needs. Once we have adequately met these needs, we can worry about meeting the needs of others.

In the early 2000s, medical schools across the nation changed the time-honored practice of having medical residents work twenty-four- and thirty-six-hour shifts, because it was becoming evident that the resulting sleep deprivation was causing major medical errors and cases of poor judgment. Most studies recommend eight hours of sleep a night, although some people will need a little more, some a little less. Whatever the amount, make sure that it is adequate, and that you get that amount of sleep consistently, going to bed more or less at the same time as often as possible to develop a pattern or habit of winding down. I also find it helps to refrain from watching television programs or reading anything that might be too stimulating or upsetting right before bed. Sometimes turning down the lights and taking some time to pray or meditate before bed not only calms the spirit but can clear the mind and give the body a subconscious cue that it's time to switch over to relaxation mode.

Rest and recreation are not frivolities that can wait for the weekend or be put off because you're dealing with someone who is sick or even dying. Each day should have some element of rest and play. Rest is any activity that calms, soothes, and relaxes us; it might be praying, taking a walk, listening to music, or even taking a catnap. Meditation and contemplation are ways to rest and give the mind down time by stopping the endless background noise and mind chatter, allowing healing and restoration to happen.

Recreation (play) is anything that is quite literally "recreative," meaning it "re-creates" us, body, mind, and spirit. Exercise, swimming, jogging, and cycling are all wonderful physical recreations. Reading, doing Sudoku or crossword puzzles, playing chess or a computer game can engage and re-energize the mind. And many other activities, such as knitting, crafting, tai chi, and yoga, can be recreative at several levels, engaging body, mind, and spirit; they can be meditative practices that are also hobbies or physical exercise.

For many of us who might be single for long periods, sex remains perhaps the most difficult need to address in an ongoing, satisfying manner. By taking a healthy and balanced approach to other needs, especially eating healthy foods and exercising, the raging hormonal push for sex can often be somewhat eased. Still, besides releasing tension and flooding our bodies with endorphins that not only create pleasure but ease pain and aid relaxation, sex can be very restorative, and a loving sexual relationship is very healing. As a chaplain, I have learned from my patients and their loved ones that sex and sexual intimacy can play an important part in how people love and relate to one another right up until the time of death.

When family members are overwhelmed caring for their dying loved ones, I often encourage them to take some time off to go out with friends or go on a "date night" with their spouse or significant other. Sometimes these family members express feelings of guilt about going out and having a good time while someone they love is sick and suffering. Sometimes that guilt centers around their need for sex and intimacy at a time when they might think this is selfish or inappropriate. It's important to remember that taking adequate care of ourselves is never selfish or inappropriate, and that sex isn't only about satisfying a physical urge. At another level it is about procreation, something we tend to forget until the time in our lives in which we start wanting to have a child. Yet, procreation is about more than having children; procreation is deeply linked to our conscious and often unconscious desire to survive beyond this life. It is our DNA's way of making sure it enters the gene pool and keeps on going.

When we are in any environment where death is so prevalent, it is important to remember that the unconscious roots of sexual desire might be telling us that we need to take a closer look at our beliefs about our own physical mortality. Being able to come to grips with the cold fact that we are merely mortal—with limited time on this plane of existence—can help us to focus our lives and prioritize our efforts. This realization can also help us value each moment given to us, here and now. And when we live more in the moment, we tend to make sure that each moment is a quality moment. Living consciously, we can live in a manner where urgency and neglect are pushed aside and where conscious, healthy living is embraced and practiced. Ironically, being aware of our mortality helps us to live better and often longer. "Now" becomes the time to take better care of our bodies and ourselves, not "some day."

Intimacy is essential to ongoing well-being, but sex is not the only means to get it. Regularly cultivating and maintaining intimate relationships with our friends and families will help us remain truly rooted in those supportive relationships when we are dealing with sickness and death. However, equally important to cultivating relationships with others is learning to enjoy being by ourselves, developing "intimacy" with the Sacred and the Mysterious. No amount of dogmatic learning or practice, be it spiritual, religious, or psychological, can replace experiential knowledge and awareness of that which lies beyond this realm of existence, and this experiential knowledge and awareness is only garnered through turning our attention toward it expectantly. In my experience, the main thing that helps people to die in peace, as well as live with purpose, is peak moments of discovery and awareness. Only when we are able to take our attention off ourselves and our own concerns can we turn expectantly towards the Mysterious and the Divine, where we will find not only sustenance for surviving whatever life throws our way but also hope and comfort in our own passing and the passing of our loved ones.

People working with the sick and the dying often put on weight, but that isn't simply about the bad food in the hospital cafeteria. Understandably, when we are very stressed or exhausted with the tasks of caregiving, we might find it difficult to find the time to prepare healthy meals and eat well, but if we are neglecting our nutritional needs on a long-term or ongoing basis, major changes in how we deal with feeding ourselves need to be made. A study in the January–February 2009 issue of the *Journal of Health Affairs* concluded that 75 percent of the country's $2.5 trillion in health-care spending has to do with four increasingly prevalent chronic diseases: obesity, Type 2 diabetes, heart disease and cancer. (Melanie Warner, "Health Care Savings Could Start in the Cafeteria." *NY Times*, November 29, 2009.) Of these four diseases, obesity and Type 2 diabetes are directly related to how we eat, and heart disease and some forms of cancer can be caused or exacerbated by what we eat. Eating properly is crucial to overall health and can very well determine the manner in which we might die.

Consciously or unconsciously, we often eat for reasons other than hunger. Many of us eat when we are stressed, and many of us eat as a means of "self-medication" or oral gratification. A case in point is illustrated by the goodies so prevalent at nursing stations and break rooms throughout hospitals. Medical personnel are often overworked, eating on the run, so having convenience food handy is one easy way caregivers eat when they can. However, the foods often found at the nursing stations are loaded with sugar and fat—cookies, brownies, potato chips, and candies—producing only a temporary hunger fix; in the long run appetite increases, and with it, an increase of the risk for diabetes and added pounds. Medical staff, more than most other people, should know the dangers of eating poorly, but the chronic stress and strain of their daily duties all too often is softened with a little bit—or a lot!—of comfort food. Remember my breakfast sausage and pancakes?

So how can we eat in a healthy manner when there is little time to prepare a good meal or when stress and exhaustion have literally immobilized us? First, it helps if we can anticipate the stress and exhaustion ahead of time, then stock up on easy-to-prepare, healthy foods that can be literally eaten on the run. Single-serving-size bags of nuts, healthy granola and snack bars, low fat cheese or peanut butter with crackers, hard-boiled eggs, or even chocolate-covered raisins or cranberries are all convenient snack foods that can satisfy the "comfort food factor" while still being relatively healthy choices.

Still, we shouldn't try to live on a diet of snacks. If we enjoy food and gain comfort and stress relief from eating, I suggest we make eating one of our recreative pastimes. By that I don't mean sitting down and eating for pleasure every chance we get. Instead, on a day off, we can indulge in shopping and purchasing food items at health-food stores and farmer's markets, take classes on healthy cooking, and spend a little extra money to eat at restaurants serving healthy food. Lots of people complain that good food is expensive and that it's cheaper to eat junk or fast food. But very often these same people have no problem buying several carbonated, sugar-laden drinks each day, getting chips out of the vending machine, or buying five dollar coffee drinks. The money we can save by getting rid of just one of these habits could finance a nice evening out at a sushi bar or a healthy restaurant every week.

Life Lessons from Caring for Marjorie

Marjorie was my patient for nearly a year and a half, during which time I watched her health spiral downward until ultimately she died from complications due to Type 2 diabetes. Like so many of us, Marjorie put weight on as she got older. With that weight gain, it became more and more difficult for her to remain active or exercise. When Marjorie's husband died, she became more housebound and sedentary, and she soon developed Type 2 diabetes. When I first saw her, she was in recovery from complications after hip-replacement surgery. Hip-replacement surgeries are often weight-related, and complications from joint-replacement surgeries are more common when patients are diabetic and overweight.

I liked Marjorie. She was clever, outgoing and very sharp. In fact, she knew everything there was to know about hip-replacement surgery, diabetes, and obesity. She was always reading up on her ailments, and she was an energetic and inquisitive participant at her own care conferences when the medical staff got together to devise a plan for her. She also threw herself into a whole slew of complementary therapies that our hospital provided, including the "humor cart," healing touch, and occupational therapy. She even requested nutritional counseling and hypnosis to help her with her tendency to overeat. As her health began to decline, she spent a lot of time with the social worker getting her legal and personal affairs in order and talking about her increasing depression. She talked with me, her chaplain, about dying.

Marjorie was Catholic, so she asked to be anointed by her parish priest; she often prayed traditional Catholic prayers and received daily communion as part of her spiritual practice. Sometimes on my visits, Marjorie would ask me to say the rosary with her, and I was happy to do so. I could see that reciting the repetitive prayers was calming, bringing her peace in the midst of all her physical ailments. Yet, as Marjorie's condition deteriorated, and her mind became more confused, new and different spiritual practices—often quite simple—brought her comfort. I usually found Marjorie holding her rosary rather than praying with it, or simply staring out the window that overlooked a beautiful courtyard full of trees and flowers. As her physical condition deteriorated, Marjorie's depression increased. Yet despite this and her dementia, she would sometimes gaze out the window into the distance with a look of peace. In the early days of her illness, Marjorie had told me that she was not "a touchy, feely type," but she now enjoyed holding hands when I came to visit. Even before she slipped into a coma, I suspect that Marjorie had lost interest in, or perhaps the ability to know, any of the particulars about me. Nevertheless, this did not inhibit her enjoyment of the simple intimacy of holding my hand.

Like Marjorie, during this time I found myself embracing a variety of spiritual practices—whatever most fit my need. When I was exhausted or especially stressed, simply sitting quietly out in nature connected me deeply to the divine in a manner that other more formal spiritual practices could not. For one thing, I simply hadn't the energy or the ability to concentrate on anything more taxing than "just being." Yet "just being" was deeply, deeply healing and restorative.

Over the next year and a half, I watched Marjorie decline in bits and pieces. She re-entered the hospital numerous times because her diabetic ulcers or her high blood pressure had got out of hand. She lost toes, and then gradually more and more of one leg, and then the other. Marjorie was becoming not only more and more debilitated, but more and more depressed. During her last six months with us, dementia gradually took hold of her mind. Ultimately, she suffered several strokes and finally lapsed into a coma and died.

Throughout Marjorie's time with us, I became very familiar with her daughter, a woman about my own age, who was Marjorie's primary caregiver. I had always liked Marjorie's sharp wit, dry sense of humor, and the warmth and appreciation she had shown our staff. However, I could see that Marjorie was an entirely different person with her daughter. Nothing the daughter tried to do for Marjorie was ever good enough, and Marjorie made sure everyone knew that. She was also quite vocal about her daughter's perceived faults, often in her daughter's company. Where I saw an attentive and caring adult daughter who was trying her best in an arguably no-win situation, Marjorie saw a selfish child who would never be good enough or meet her standards. Predictably, the two got along like oil and water, and much of the time Marjorie's daughter was angry, frustrated, hurt, and very tired.

I like to think that if I were Marjorie's daughter, I would have walked away from this situation, but our ties to loved ones are deep and complicated. Marjorie's daughter stuck it out, trying her best to help her mother despite her ingratitude. The daughter did what most people do as a situation degenerates— she increased her time, care, and attention. Yet, she also needed more time to take care of herself. Sometimes, running around doing all kinds of things for the sick and dying is a way to deny what's going on. Marjorie's daughter revealed to me that, predictably, they hadn't had the best mother-daughter relationship in the world. She was unconsciously trying to fix the relationship in its last days by overcompensating with her care of her mother. I reminded her that we cannot fix the universe. In fact, more often than not, we need to step away from the universe. I encouraged her to grab a date night with her somewhat neglected husband, including dinner and a movie if possible. I invited her to go home and indulge in any kind of restorative behavior—hot baths with scented bath salts, restful music and flickering votive candles, or whatever worked for her.

All my patients have had something to teach me, but I would have preferred another way for Marjorie to impart so many very important life lessons; as it was, I had to learn by watching the unsettling consequences of how she chose to live. I saw before me the realities of not eating and exercising well, and the end results were not pretty. In fact, I was so upset by watching Marjorie's slow spiral downward that I went home and joined a health club so I could swim laps year round. I also wound up cutting out my morning "mocha lattes" at the coffee shop and cut back on fried foods and late night snacks. I wound up losing fifteen pounds.

Despite being a strong-willed and outgoing woman, Marjorie was lost without her husband of nearly fifty years. In fact, she often told me that after her husband's death, she simply didn't care to keep going anymore, and that preparing good meals or taking a walk were too much trouble, or too lonely.

I love my husband very much, but, watching Marjorie, I realized that I did not want to be so debilitated if I lost him that I would cease to care for myself. We often have a rather romanticized notion about people dying of a broken heart, and I believe this does happen. Yet more often than not, we do not immediately follow our loved ones in death. We can choose to abdicate life by self neglect, but this kind of decline is not a pretty affair. The importance of developing and maintaining a strong community of supportive relationships—beyond my husband—was a hard lesson I learned from Marjorie and from working in health care.

There was another difficult lesson. While socially adept at putting her best face forward to the public, Marjorie was not pleasant with her family. Frankly, I could not understand why it was so important to Marjorie that her daughter think and act like her, and I used to go home from work very sad at having witnessed a mother and daughter play out the last months of the mother's life in such a sad and unfulfilling series of exchanges. It bothered me so much that I had to sit down and really look at the situation. Finally I realized that I, too, have a tendency to set high standards—or at least *my* standards!—and I often make demands upon others to think and act like me, especially with my husband. I had a choice, I realized. I could continue to waste precious years trying to change him—hurting and alienating him in the process, or I could accept him. Our loved ones deserve our indulgent and affectionate regard, not our efforts to constantly remake them in our own image. That was a hard lesson Marjorie taught me.

Finally, watching Marjorie's dying was taxing for me and for the rest of the staff, because it took so long and was such a thorough and pernicious decline. Dealing with Marjorie brought home the importance of ongoing self-care, and I learned how to deal with stress in a variety of ways. Like her daughter, I needed to step away from the universe every now and then. I went for regular massages and took long walks in nature. I had monthly appointments with a spiritual companion—a kind of life coach of the spirit—who would listen to me and help me process some of the issues that came up in dealing with my patients and their families. I spent a lot of time in prayer and meditation, stopping off in the hospital chapel for a breather when I was feeling overwhelmed or needed to re-center myself. And I developed good and supportive relationships with the nurses, nursing assistants, and housekeepers on my units—relationships that were happy, positive, and mutually beneficial.

In the end, Marjorie and her daughter experienced a healing of sorts. As Marjorie's mind became more and more demented, her daughter came and sat with her mother, holding hands with few words exchanged. A shift in how the two related to each other occurred, and Marjorie's daughter experienced a new level of peace and acceptance around who her mother had been, as well as around her own relationship with her mother with all its ups and downs.

In situations of sickness, desperation, and suffering, the best way spiritual caregivers can help others is to show them another way to live, right up through the moment of death. And the only way we can really show others another way to live is to embody that other way of living ourselves.

Chapter Four

LEARNING TO LISTEN

K EISHA WAS BROUGHT INTO THE EMERGENCY ROOM bruised and bleeding, yet conscious after an automobile accident. She was immediately wheeled into a cubicle where the medical team lifted her off the gurney and onto the hospital bed. They frantically tried to cut away Keisha's clothing in order to assess her injuries. Yet, instead of cooperating with the medical staff as we would have hoped and expected, Keisha began screaming and fighting them off, risking further injury to herself and the staff. The chief resident-in-charge, a young man whom, until this moment, I hadn't particularly liked, had the presence of mind to shout, "Stop!"—to the astonishment of the medical team. Then locking eyes with me, he ordered, "You!" pointing at me and then pointing to the patient.

While the medical team drew back, I approached the bed. Keisha was panting and trembling, barely able to keep her hysteria at bay. Suddenly, it occurred to me why this young woman might be having such an extreme reaction. Here she was, an African American woman in an ER after a traumatic encounter, surrounded by a largely white medical team shouting and ripping her clothing off. As a European American, I view white people such as myself as largely benign individuals, most of whom deplore racism and racial injustice. Yet years ago, when I went to work for a historically black college as one of the few white staff members, I found, in listening to our black students and staff, that the majority of them did not assume the best about white people. In fact, I was often told in so many words that "white folk" had to prove where they stood on various issues through their actions, not their words; they had to be observed interacting with blacks over the long haul; a few superficial interactions proved nothing. Only after such scrutiny would blacks accept white people in any serious manner. I also listened to many stories of rape and lynching. To me this sounded almost like ancient history, but to my fellow staff and students, the stories recounted wounds that were present and raw, warranting mistrust and precaution among blacks when dealing with the "majority culture." I did not like what I heard, but I heard it so many times that I had to come to terms with the fact that for many of my students and fellow staff, this was their reality—their worldview.

So, it was with this perspective that I could see that for this young black woman, the sudden and seemingly aggressive actions of a white mob—because that is perhaps what we looked like to her—shouting orders and ripping at her clothing, might have stirred up her historical DNA, or even terrifying personal memories, past injuries, injustices, and assaults suffered by her, her loved ones, and her people. I took Keisha's hand in mine and, following my hunch, said to her, "I'm Karen, the medical team's chaplain. No one here is going to hurt you. I promise." Immediately Keisha relaxed, but then something even more amazing happened. The medical team went back to cutting off the woman's clothing, but in a gentle and slow manner, even speaking more softly to her and to one another. One of the nurses followed my lead and took Keisha's hand in hers and offered her soothing words and support. The whole dynamic of the situation quickly changed. Now everyone had listened to and understood a new reality.

This particular incident also changed how the ER staff related to me and the services I could provide as a chaplain in the midst of such trauma situations. Though the chief resident and I never became "friends," we now at least acknowledged each other with respect and as peers. We no longer treated each other warily and arrogantly with harbored biases—his view of the stereotypical "goodie-goodie" but rather useless chaplain and my view of the "rude and abrupt know-it-all resident."

Working with the sick and dying, I have learned that few skills are more important to have and to cultivate than the ability to listen and, particularly, to be able to listen at a variety of levels. Listening goes way beyond merely taking the time to consciously turn our full attention to what the sick and dying are saying. Anyone who wants to spiritually care for others, particularly the sick and dying, needs to also learn how to listen to what's *not* being said. We need to listen to the unconscious biases, fears, assumptions, and presumptions that we as well as others hold, and learn how to distance ourselves in a manner that can help us "listen" to what's going on at a deeper level. This is the kind of "listening" that helped me help a frightened young African American patient, whose worldview and assumptions were perhaps in many areas radically different from my own or the other members of our medical team.

Spiritual caregivers also need to develop "deep listening," nurturing and trusting not only our intuitions—those "flashes" of insight and inspiration that come to us suddenly—but learning to honor and embrace the often mysterious and confusing language the dying speak. And in order to be spiritual healers who truly heal more than harm, we must learn to be attentive to subtler, deeper forms of communication and healing available for both the psyche and soul.

Learning to Listen at a Deeper Level

I was once called to an Intensive Care Unit to bless an empty room. This is not a typical request to a chaplain, so I sought out someone at the nursing station to tell me what was going on. The nurses exchanged embarrassed smirks and told me to "Go find Denise." Denise, whom I knew as a competent and dedicated nurse, was visibly shaken when she told me that the last six patients who had inhabited that particular room had died, and she felt the room was either "cursed" or "haunted." The "bad spirits" residing there needed to be exorcised.

Now, I was pretty busy that particular shift, and I could have just blessed the room and left a note at the nursing station saying I'd accomplished the order, but I knew the importance of finding out the root cause of the request by listening to the person who had made it. I learned from Denise that her deeper concerns went beyond an ICU room she perceived as "cursed." Listening to both what Denise was and wasn't saying, I was able to hear that Denise's very image of herself, as a competent, logical person who takes good care of her patients, was threatened by this unusual situation. Denise was not a person who embraced paranormal experiences as a given, and now she was faced with a troubling and menacing string of deaths, all in the same room; she seriously wondered if it was more than mere coincidence. As a nurse—a person devoted to caring for the well-being of others—she felt helpless in the face of a series of events she did not understand and could not control.

So, I blessed the room, but I also did two other things: first, I gave Denise a workable format for future blessings that she could embrace or alter and do herself; and, second, I invited Denise to participate in that blessing. Denise took a small bottle of scented oil and with it made a sign of blessing on each of the four walls of the room, while I recited a blessing, asking that this room continue to be a place of healing for the patients and families it would house in the future, and that any negative energy be banished. Inviting Denise to bless the room honored her fears and frustrations, but also underscored her desire to serve life and heal others.

Another time, I was called back to the intensive care unit in the middle of the night to deal with the family member of a patient who was exhibiting "threatening behavior." When I arrived, the security guards were trying to lead a man out of the ICU in what looked like a situation of escalating threat and unpleasantness; in fact, the man, David, was beginning to scream in rage and frustration while, in response, the security guards became more and more aggressive and authoritarian.

I managed to get the security guards to wait outside the room while I spoke with David. After he was able to calm down, David explained to me that although it was two in the morning, he had actually just got off a plane to rush to his dying mother's bedside, only to find that she had been intubated (meaning a breathing tube had been put down her throat) despite her ardent wishes never to be put on life support. She wanted to be allowed to die in peace after a long and lingering illness. David, seeing his mother with a tube down her throat, demanded that the nurses remove the tube. The nurses balked and said that could not be done in the middle of the night without a doctor's order. Initially David appeared to me and the medical team to be disproportionately upset, which triggered the nurse's suspicion that something was amiss with the situation. Yet when David explained that he had repeatedly promised his mother that he would never let a tube be put down her throat and here she was intubated after what apparently was for him a long, tiring flight in the middle of the night, his protestations made more sense. In this man's eyes, he had unwittingly broken his promise to his mother and was suffering tremendous anguish at his inability to abide by her wishes. Although it was the middle of the night, we found a doctor to come in and review the medical notes and talk with David and ultimately extubate the woman while her son held her hand. With tears streaming down his face, David told his mother that he had indeed made sure her wishes were followed . . . that she could go in peace, even though he loved her and would miss her terribly.

Listening to Our Intuition

One of the most accurate and powerful sources of guidance we can receive is through intuition. When honored, it is also a type of listening that can be developed as a tool that, with practice, comes more frequently and accurately.

I was called in to deal with a new patient, Bertha, who was very agitated. Bertha was an elderly woman who had been admitted to our hospital in the last stages of a terminal illness. The nurses were upset because Bertha was fighting everything they were trying to do to take care of her, and, in fact, when they tried explaining to her that they were only trying to help her, she fought them harder, slapping their hands and trying to get out of bed.

Something about the situation spoke to me, and, intuitively, I felt that the issue at hand was that this woman in the last stages of her illness was actually afraid that she was going to be "helped"—helped by being "kept alive" by "helpful nurses" when all she wanted was the relief from her sufferings that death would bring. So, going by a strong gut feeling, I sat down and took Bertha's hand and told her not to worry, that we were not going to do anything extraordinary to extend her life or intervene in any manner, and that we would take good care of her and keep her as pain free as we possibly could until her time came. I got out my prayer book and began reciting Psalm 23, a prayer that most Christians facing death resonate with, as Bertha's medical chart stated she was Methodist. Immediately Bertha became calm and peaceful, to the astonishment of one of the nurses who later said to me, "I would have never thought that basically telling an agitated patient, 'Don't worry, we're going to let you die,' would actually work to calm them down!"

In another scenario, a nurse and I were called to the home of a new hospice patient to get her enrolled in our program. Something about the situation just didn't feel right, particularly the way the patient's husband—the stepfather of her three teen-aged girls—looked at two of the girls, and how they did not return eye contact, but seemed skittish and uncomfortable around him. Returning from the home visit, I told the nurse worker that I had a bad feeling about the situation, and that I felt, in addition to having a dying mother of teen-aged girls to care for, we might have a situation that was complicated—if not outright abusive—sexually. The nurse, trained to deal in concrete realities, challenged me to present her with what evidence I had of this suspicion. All I could say was that from watching the dynamics in front of me, I had a strong intuition that something wasn't right. Because we couldn't do anything concrete based on a hunch—and certainly we would not have wanted to make so damaging an accusation without any evidence—we spoke with the caseworker regarding my hunch. I asked her to keep it in mind when she interviewed the girls separately at a later date. The caseworker eventually discovered that two of the three girls were, in fact, being molested by their stepfather—a situation that apparently their dying mother had known about, but felt unwilling or unable to address.

Acknowledging Our Fears, Biases, and Assumptions

I was called to help the nursing staff with a patient, Tiffany, whose newborn baby had just died. Several of the nurses were quite upset, telling me that this woman was crazy; she insisted on taking her dead baby home with her. They had tried to explain to Tiffany that this could not be done, that protocol had to be followed, and the baby would be sent to the funeral home. Nevertheless, Tiffany was insistent that her other children, who were three, five, and eight, have the opportunity to spend some time and "meet" their deceased sibling. Thus, she wanted to be discharged from the hospital accompanied by her dead baby. The nurses were suspicious of how calm Tiffany was in explaining her desire that the children all meet each other; surely she couldn't be sane, or she was just shy of some sort of breakdown, because who could be so calm after the death of a child? Their own bias was that someone that calm and articulate after the death of their baby could not possibly be a good mother. And who on earth would bring a dead baby home for little children to meet? Therefore Tiffany wasn't well, and the nurses feared she would do damage to her other children; they actually wanted me to get a social worker involved in investigating if the mother was a fit parent.

I have seen many, many deaths and dealt with many, many families in the immediate aftermath, and I can tell you that there is no "normal" way to react to death. Thus, I didn't harbor the same "assumptions" the nurses did regarding Tiffany, based on a supposed lack of displayed grief; I know that even the most loving family members are able to summon such extraordinary presence of mind in the midst of heartbreaking tragedy that it might make them appear "cold" or unfeeling. Other equally loving people fall completely apart. Neither response is better than the other in the long run.

When I talked to Tiffany, several things came to light besides her supposed "calm" manner in the midst of her child's death. First of all, she had come into the hospital expecting to deliver a deceased infant because her doctor discovered what Tiffany had already suspected and dreaded—that the baby's heart had stopped beating. So, Tiffany had had several days to prepare for the "loss" of her child. What's more, she only asked to be able to take the remains of her child from the hospital when it was made clear to her, after several requests, that her children would not be allowed into the hospital to see their departed baby sibling. What Tiffany really wanted was for the children to be let into the hospital to be able to see and hold the baby, not necessarily to take it home with her.

Tiffany explained to me that when she was a child, her own mother went to the hospital to have a baby, but then came home without one. What had happened to the baby was never discussed, although as a child Tiffany believed that somehow her ambivalence about having a new sister or brother probably caused the baby's death. Also, the consequences of that suppressed and unarticulated grief had weighed heavily on the entire family the rest of their lives. Tiffany did not want the same burden for her children. They had expected a sibling, and she felt it would help them grieve in the short term as well as in the long to have the same privilege and comfort she had had, namely, the opportunity to view the baby and say good-bye.

My own bias was that Tiffany's children were too young to deal with the situation. But in the end, I feel my role as a chaplain is to suspend my value system in favor of what the patient or family members believe in their hearts to be the ultimate good. In other words, I'm not there to judge them; I am there to listen to them, to help them review their options, and make the best decision they feel able to make.

When I explained to the nursing staff Tiffany's need—and right—to help her other children process the baby's death, many of them were still against having children that young on the medical recovery floor to view a body.

In the end, we struck a compromise. We moved Tiffany to a private room where her husband was able to bring the three children, and we prepared the baby's body for the viewing. This might sound morbid, but there are many things that can be done to prepare a baby's body for viewing and holding by loved ones, including washing, dressing, and even warming the body slightly by laying the baby in a portable incubator. We even applied baby powder to the tiny body to help fend off some of the odors already setting in. In the end, my own assumptions were challenged—assumptions that small children could not emotionally handle a death. The children all held the child gently and tenderly, without tears or terror, and said their good-byes. Tiffany explained that the baby had wanted to join their family but, through no one's fault, was unable to stay with them and had to "go back to be with God." They actually named the baby together as a family and were able to hug and kiss their little sibling good-bye.

All of us have fears, biases, and assumptions that we have acquired over a lifetime, and often they can inhibit our abilities to give good care to our patients and their families. We who are healers are all "wounded healers," to quote the great spiritual writer Henri Nouwen. It might help us to remember that we and everyone else spend a lifetime recovering from the wounds of living. We need to be gentle with ourselves and others, yet mindful that we may inadvertently hurt each other because of these wounds.

So, what's a caregiver to do? One could become paralyzed realizing the sobering ability we each have to wound others. I would suggest a couple of things. First, despite the wounds each of us sustains—or inflicts!—life can and will present us with untold opportunities to heal and be healed. We can take comfort in knowing that any hurt we have done—intentionally or unintentionally—is not beyond healing. People often find peace and healing in spite of us, not because of us. Also, by becoming more conscious of our inner wounds, we are less likely to act unconsciously out of our "wounded-ness." As caregivers, we can open ourselves to the possibility of deep healing for ourselves and others by adopting an attitude of radical "listening" for divine action to move around and within us and others. Prayer, meditation, contemplation—these are all ways in which we can be still and empty ourselves, and attempt to listen and accept this radical healing power that does not have its origins in ourselves.

Taking the Risk to Listen Deeply

I will reiterate what I said in Chapter 1: I believe risk-taking is the single most important factor that determines whether we live a good life and die a good death. In order to know what risks to take and to be able to take the right risks, we need to listen to our own heart, to the guidance of others, to the situation at hand, to what life has to show us, and to what is revealed to us in loving relationship with the Divine and the universe. This type of listening takes time and intention so that we can discern our "life's assignment."

Moses, Jesus, Mohammed, Siddhartha Gautama, and perhaps the most well-known Hindu of our time, Gandhi, all spent time listening "in the desert."

Each took time from daily life to discern what wound up being their "life's assignments." Each made outreaches of profound healing, whether that healing was the physical kind Jesus performed for the sick, or helping people escape from and heal from the afflictions of slavery, discrimination, poverty, human ignorance, and suffering.

Every major religion and spiritual path recognizes the importance of listening. Adherents of Hinduism practice various forms of yoga, practices that can aid them in achieving deep meditation and listening. Moses fled to the desert, where he found God prior to returning to Egypt, to lead the Jewish people into freedom. Siddhartha Gautama, regarded as the supreme "Buddha" or "enlightened one," fled the privileges of the palace to contemplate human suffering and seek enlightenment. Jesus fasted and prayed for forty days in the desert prior to beginning his ministry. Mohammed retreated into a cave in the desert where he encountered God in order to gain wisdom. Many of the indigenous spiritualities emphasize vision quests or shamanic practice—times apart from the community to receive revelation and inspiration.

In my opinion, the most helpful kind of listening we can cultivate is prayer of some sort, especially silent meditation or contemplation, which have a way of healing the psyche and opening our hearts at levels rational thinking or discursive knowledge cannot provide. When we stop speaking and start listening attentively, our attitudes, perspectives, and even our talents and abilities will start to shift. I know a couple of chaplains who say that they have worked with death so long, they can now often recognize it as a "felt presence" that enters the hospital room, and frankly I don't have any trouble believing that. Remember the Grim Reaper? Ever wonder if there wasn't a reason our ancestors, who dealt personally and face to face with frequent death, portrayed death in such a precise way as a being or presence?

Cultivating listening skills will also help us listen to a very important but often overlooked resource for discernment and knowledge—our dreams. Several health-care workers have told me that they have had dreams that revealed to them the answer to a particular problem for their patients and families. A friend of mine who is a doctor even told me that one of her dreams helped her diagnose a patient the medical team had been unable to help. She made me promise that I would never reveal who she is because, she claims, "If my patients knew I was taking cues from my dreams, that would probably be the end of my medical practice."

The Thin Place Between Life and Death

Anyone who works with the dying long enough knows that the dying get to a point when what they are saying often doesn't "make sense," and no amount of "listening" at a rational level can help us help them. I would strongly recommend to anyone working, or contemplating working, with the dying that they look at the book, *When the Dying Speak: How to Listen to and Learn from Those Facing Death,* by Ron Wooten Green. Many of us are familiar with the term "near-death experience" (or NDE) coined by the Swiss-born psychiatrist Elisabeth Kübler-Ross. (We will talk about that in the following chapter.) Wooten Green speaks of another reality known as "nearing death awareness," which relates to how the dying perceive their changing landscape and communicate it to us. "Nearing death awareness" is the stage when a dying patient begins to become aware of and interact with a world that you and I cannot see. When interacting with that world, people often use language that to our ears is indirect, pointing, almost metaphorically, to realities larger than they are able to verbally articulate.

My husband embraces the Irish notion of the "thin place," a space between life in this world and the next. The "thin place" is a place in Irish and Celtic spirituality that tentatively connects the two worlds that can open up mysteriously and without bidding or warning as the dying begin their journey from this world to the next. Dying individuals can remain in or move in and out of the thin space for minutes, hours, days, or weeks. Each journey is unique to the individual, as is the language each individual uses to describe what he or she sees and experiences in this thin place. Dying individuals experiencing "nearing death awareness" may appear to be speaking in metaphor about death, but what they are trying to convey to us is their actual experience, sounding to us like nothing but metaphors, or more precisely, "archetypal images."

Having worked on a hospice team, I am aware that many of my cowork-ers do not believe in nearing death awareness. They believe that these episodes are merely hallucinations caused by what one doctor friend calls "meds or mets"—that is, the side effects of strong, pain-killing medications, or metas-tases, or tumors in the brain. I frankly believe in the veracity of "nearing death awareness" from my observations of patients reacting to these occurrences. Usually afterwards, they are less fearful, far more calm, and have come to a certain peace about their imminent deaths. They seem to gain something and come to a certainty about their experience that I don't believe mere hallucina-tions could produce. So, I believe it is important to listen to and honor the dying person's words and experience, regardless of what your beliefs are.

A few chapters back, I spoke about my patient Mildred, who hadn't spoken to her brother in twenty years and was having recurring dreams about a bright light beckoning her, but she couldn't reach it because there was a big wall in the way. Mildred made it clear that her experience wasn't *like* having a big wall between her and the light; there literally was a wall separating her from the light—a wall that she needed to learn to traverse.

As caregivers of the soul, we need to listen to people's experience without trying to judge or even figure it out. Our role is to listen respectfully, resist-ing the urge to insert our doubts or misgivings into the conversation; in this manner we can aid the patient in figuring out what is going on. Patients will eventually tell us what they are experiencing and what it means to them. If we want to be good caregivers—if we want to gain wisdom and insight into the mysteries of death, dying, and the possibilities of an existence beyond this one—we must listen to the mysterious language of the dying, holding their words in our hearts to ponder and treasure, giving witness to what they expe-rience, and realizing that doing so is our privilege. Listening is a skill that we will spend a lifetime learning and refining. We can begin now, as part of our self-care regime, to take the time every day to really listen. We can listen to our loved ones, to the wisdom of our spiritual path, to the divine as revealed in music, art, and nature, and the deep stirrings of our very heart.

Chapter Five

EMBRACING THE UNKNOWN

"Y OU'LL SEE," THE NURSE SAID WITH A SMIRK and a roll of her eyes. "She's not all there. You'll figure out what's going on when you get in there." This was the rather unsettling report the nurse gave me with her request that I visit a patient on our oncology unit. Upon entering the patient's room, I found Valerie, a thirty-nine-year-old woman whose medical chart indicated that she was in the advanced stages of cervical cancer. She was sitting up in bed, lively and alert, her eyes fixed on the far corner of the room.

"Are you the chaplain?" Valerie asked. "Good, the nurse thought you could help me, as none of the nursing staff seem to know what to do about this cat."

"Cat?" I asked, following the direction of her stare to the far corner of the room where, sure enough, there was no cat to be seen.

"Yes, this cat," Valerie replied, shuddering irritably. "This evil cat. It walked into my room about an hour ago and has just been sitting there staring at me. It's really freaking me out and it's got to go, but when I tell it to leave, it just continues sitting there and staring at me." Then Valerie looked over at me, and her countenance turned from one of annoyance to one of fear. "Frankly, I think it's here to hurt me, but no one is taking me seriously. Can you please help me?"

"Don't worry," I told her. "I will do my best to help you get rid of this cat. How about this? Together, we'll say a prayer and then bless this room to see if that gets rid of the cat. What do you think?"

"Yes, let's try that," said Valerie, looking somewhat relieved.

And that's precisely what we did. We told the cat—and any other menacing force that might be lurking about—that they were not welcome in this room anymore. Then, I said some prayers with Valerie—ones from her faith tradition that were comforting and familiar to her. Next, I invited her to say some prayers of her own while I made a sign of blessing on each of the walls, claiming the room as a place of peace and inner healing for the dying patient.

"Thank you," Valerie said. "The cat is gone. Now I can rest." She heaved an enormous sigh, eased back into her pillow, and, assured that she could call a chaplain to repeat the ritual if the cat returned, she drifted off to sleep.

Honoring Each Person's Unique and Mysterious Journey

We may not believe in evil forces, especially evil forces that show up looking like a house cat. We may not believe in nearing death awareness, when the dying begin to see and experience realities most other people cannot see or hear, or we might think nearing death awareness consists simply of hallucinations or the side-effects of drugs, anesthesia, or metastasis to the brain. We might find the idea of blessing a person, a room, or anything else to be a quaint or crazy relic of days gone by or simply repugnant to our own spirituality; we might even think reciting traditional prayers is mumbo jumbo at best and a poor substitute for heartfelt, spontaneous prayer, meditation, reciting affirmations, or a positive attitude. However, what is important to know is that in caring spiritually for the sick and dying, what we believe, to some degree, is a moot point.

I have learned that each and every individual is on a precious life journey that is unique; that journey will play out in a manner that is peculiar to the primary participant—each precious and unique individual. This last point may seem obvious, but think of the implications. If each of us is on a unique journey, each of us will have a different experience and a different response to that experience.

Each of us will find comfort, strength, forgiveness, and inner healing—if we are open to it—not because we were "good people" or did lots of random acts of kindness or attended a place of worship or meditation—church, temple, mosque, or Buddhist *sangha*—or did yoga on a regular basis and became all nice and enlightened. In my experience, it isn't tit for tat.

Each of us will be helped through the process—by others, by God, the universe, or whatever ultimate reality we believe in, even by our own inner resources—if we are open to it and simply because we *are* . . . simply because we exist.

I believe this because of what the dying have shown me time after time. I am convinced that each and every one of us has within or around us whatever we need to get through any adversity that life presents. And each and every one of us is loved and lovable, no matter what we have or haven't done in life. At the end of life—in our final days—the forces running the universe just want to continue doing what they've been trying to do all our lives, only more so— extend to us their love and healing. We just need to be open to it.

The dying have also taught me that a caregiver's role is to help patients with what they believe, what they believe is happening, what they believe might "work," and what they believe is an effective means of traversing the spiritual realities of this world and the next. When we are invited to share our beliefs with a patient, then and only then is it appropriate for us to do so. It also doesn't matter whether we believe in a "next world," or that everything ends with the last breath, or that there are miracles. If a patient needs to believe in the option of this life continuing in some manner after death, it is not our role or place to take that "belief" or that "hope" away.

Elisabeth Kübler-Ross, the famous physician who worked with the dying and developed the five stages of dying, has been quoted as saying that she did not believe in an afterlife until she began working with the dying, at which point she became certain of its existence (*On Death and Dying*). I, too, would say that the one thing the dying have taught me is that our lives continue in some manner on some other plane of existence after we die. You can call it Heaven or Nirvana or whatever you like, but I have seen and heard simply too much from too many patients and families to deny the existence of a life beyond this one.

Glimpses Beyond This Life

Remember, awhile back, the dying man Tom who came into our hospice unit simply terrified, until a "beautiful woman" appeared to him in his room and told him that within twenty-four hours she'd return to take him home with her? I had another patient from Ghana, Amadou, a man I visited at home at the request of his sister who was taking care of him. The sister used to beg me to come, saying a visit from the chaplain would do her brother good, but Amadou was so deeply depressed to be dying that he was almost totally unresponsive during my visits—or at any point for that matter—according to his heartbroken sister. On my last visit, shortly before Amadou died, something remarkable happened. While I was praying with him, Amadou's face suddenly lit up in joy and wonder, his eyes locked on something over my shoulder. I turned to see what he was staring at, but I could see nothing remarkable. "Do you see her? Do you see the beautiful woman?" said Amadou.

Of course I couldn't see anyone, but I asked Amadou what the woman looked like and what she was saying. He "tisked" his tongue at me, as if to say wasn't the answer obvious, but then he added, "She is Ghanaian, like me. Those are Ghanaian robes she is wearing." And then a beautiful smile of deep relief spread over his face. "She's telling me to fear no evil. Fear no evil." Initially this struck me as an odd thing to say, and not particularly comforting. I myself would have preferred "I'll be taking you home with me soon" or something to that effect, but for whatever reason, this man needed to hear that "evil" was not something to be "feared," and it was those words he received and the words that brought him peace.

Elisabeth Kübler-Ross introduced the world to the concept of the near-death experience. Working with the sick and dying, I, too, have heard of the NDEs of many individuals, and not all of them patients. I received a request to go pray with Sherry, a woman who was in recovery after having coded on the operating table during heart surgery. Actually, Sherry didn't really want to pray at all. What

Sherry really wanted was to get someone to come visit her so she could talk about her NDE. Of course, she didn't call it that, but what she told me was that she suddenly woke up during her operation and found "herself" floating above her body, looking on while the medical team frantically tried to revive her. Sherry spoke of feeling delightfully happy, light, free of pain, and able to hear everything going on in the room, including, she believed, the medical team's thoughts! "One of the nurses," she told me in awe, "was praying for me! I couldn't believe that this stranger, in the midst of all the chaos, had the presence of mind to actually say a prayer for me! But you know," she went on, suddenly looking a bit sheepish, "I felt so good, and I could feel something tugging at me gently as if it was time to go somewhere, and somewhere really good . . . I just really, really wanted to go. I almost wanted to tell the medical team, 'Look, don't bother, I'm fine, just leave that old body alone.' Then, at that very moment, I felt myself right back in my body—and boy, did it ever hurt to be back!"

I have had any number of patients tell me about their NDEs, and most of them share the same characteristics of coming out of their bodies, feeling joyful and free, being pulled into a tunnel filled with bright light or into a tunnel with bright light at the end of it. Most patients with NDEs lose much of their fear of dying, and many go on to change the way they live. I know, because many of those people ultimately became involved in hospice and hospital work and some of them are my friends.

I am not going to expound about NDEs because I think they are a fairly well-known, well-documented phenomenon. But I will share one particularly poignant experience when I was called to the bedside of a perplexed and baffled patient to help with what wound up being a classic NDE.

After hearing the details of the event, I took the patient's hand and exclaimed, "Wow, what an experience you've had! Isn't that wonderful?" whereupon the patient yanked her hand from mine and nearly spat.

"No it's not wonderful! Don't you understand that I don't believe in any of that crap?!"

Whether she believed it or not, here was this poor patient with a new experience to process.

Communicating with Our Loved Ones After Death

A person who wants to give spiritual care to the sick and the dying must be willing to become comfortable with working with mystery . . . and with the unknown. We might not have the answer to everything; in fact, we might not have the answer to much. But having answers is not what is important. What is important is being willing to journey fearlessly and lovingly with the sick and dying and to share what we believe and have experienced. Only when our beliefs and experience are *asked for* should they be shared, and at a time when our opinions won't hurt or compromise the patient in any manner, and only if valuing and affirming the patient's own beliefs and life experiences.

One of the best books on the subject of spiritual care of the dying is *Final Gifts: Understanding the Special Awareness, Needs and Communication of the Dying*, written by two hospice nurses, Maggie Callanan and Patricia Kelley. Published in 1992, the book is still in print, and I recommend it highly. Like Kübler-Ross's *On Death and Dying*, this book is a classic for anyone caring for the dying and their loved ones. Maggie Callanan went on to write another book, *Final Journeys: A Practical Guide for Bringing Care and Comfort at the End of Life*, in which she talks about "After-Death Communications" (ADCs), another phenomenon experienced around death. Ron Wooten Green talks about the same phenomenon, calling it "near-life experiences."

Let me share a couple of examples of ADCs. A girlfriend of mine, Gail, was missing her mother terribly as the rest of the family gathered to celebrate their first "Thanksgiving without Mom." After dinner, while much of the family retreated to the living room to watch a football game, Gail found herself sitting all alone at the dining room table, missing her mother and overwhelmed by the melancholy of an aching heart. Almost immediately the radio, which someone had turned on without my friend realizing it, began playing Gail's mother's favorite song.

"When I heard that song," she explained, "I got goose bumps. But I also felt flooded with comfort—that kind of comfort only my mother used to be able to give me. I know you'll think this is silly or that the song playing at that particular moment was just a coincidence, but I really and truly believe that song was my mother's doing and that somehow she was letting me know that she was OK and missing me, too."

Once an elderly patient, Doris, spoke to me of missing terribly her husband of fifty-five years after he died. Then, almost furtively, Doris confessed, "I know you'll just think I'm going batty, but do you know that sometimes I hear him calling me? He used to have this annoying habit," and she laughed, "of calling me from the den—'Hey, Doris, come see this!' or 'Hey, Doris, how about a snack?' Of course, now that he's gone, what I wouldn't give to be 'annoyed' in that manner again! But you know, every now and then I'll be sitting home, watching the TV or reading, and I'll hear him clear as day call, 'Hey, Doris!' The first couple times it happened I ran all over the house looking for him, thinking I was losing my mind. Now, when I hear him every now and then, I don't go looking for him, but neither do I think I'm crazy. *You* might think I'm crazy, but I know that it's just *him* checking in on me."

Trudy Harris, a former hospice nurse and the president of the Hospice Foundation for Caring shares inspiring stories based on her years in the field of caring for the dying in her book, *Glimpses of Heaven: True Stories of Hope and Peace at the End of Life's Journey*. One of my favorite stories from Trudy's book illustrates poignantly how often our actions can unwittingly bring "supernatural" comfort to patients and their families experiencing a traumatic death. She tells the story of a nurse who, on the way to visit a couple whose hospice-patient child had just died, stopped and picked up a single yellow rose for the family without even really understanding why she felt compelled to do so. The nurse had no way of knowing that the couple considered yellow roses a special sign or symbol of God's love and care for them. Even more amazing, a friend of the couple sent them a rosebush for their garden shortly after the death of their child. Every year in February, on the anniversary of their child's death, a single yellow rose blooms on that bush.

Similarly, I worked with a family whose one-year-old child, having been born severely disabled and after surviving months of complications and setbacks, eventually died. The little child's mother, Amanda, loved deer and thought of deer as "special messengers" of divine love and care; she even had a couple of cement deer statues scattered across her front lawn. When the family went to the cemetery for their child's burial, a single deer emerged from the woods and came over and stood mere yards from the family throughout the entire service. When the service was over, the deer simply turned around and walked back into the woods. Amanda later told me that this single incident did more to bring her strength, comfort, and healing than anything else she was to experience after her child's death.

Accepting Life's Mysteries

Sometimes they're called mysteries, sometimes they're called miracles. They are "that which cannot be explained," a suspension of the normal laws of nature, an unexpected, unforeseen, and unexplainable change in circumstances, paranormal experience, or whatever you want to call them. The Suncoast Hospice, one of the nation's biggest hospices, cites paranormal experience in the form of visions, hearing voices, and sensing the presence of departed loved ones or spiritual beings as "experiences (sic) common as death approaches." (N.A, "Spiritual Care: The Hospice of the Florida Suncoast," 1996, p. 106.) The hospice organization consciously develops sensitivity to their existence in the training of its personnel. Citing that hospice professionals regularly observe spiritual experience in the lives of hospice patients and families, the organization found that a significant outcome of these spiritual experiences is a degree of healing integration of the physical, sensory, emotional, psychological, and religious dimensions of life (*Guidelines for Spiritual Care in Hospice*, National Hospice Organization). Whatever the phenomenon and wherever it originates, the events will challenge our assumptions and forever change how we will look at "reality."

I was once chaplain to an eighty-four-year old African American woman, Betty, who had Stage 4 breast cancer, meaning the cancer had spread throughout her body to her vital organs—a terminal prognosis. In other words, her doctor told Betty she was going to die. However, Betty's cancer mysteriously and suddenly went into complete remission, so complete, in fact, that the doctors couldn't find any indication of it anywhere on the numerous X-rays they took. The hospice medical team was flabbergasted, but Betty was very pragmatic. "Honey," she told me, "it just wasn't my time yet. In the meantime, I'm just thanking and praising God."

Once, at the request of family members, I went to a comatose patient's room in the Intensive Care Unit. For about five minutes, I sat at Cora's bedside and said a silent prayer. After more than an hour consoling the distraught family in the waiting room, I knew quite a bit about her situation, including how very upset her eight-year-old grandson was at the prospect of losing his grandmother. So I added a quick intention for him into my silent litany of prayers for her.

Two weeks later, I went to visit Cora just after she had emerged from her coma. Although the only time we had "met" was while she had been in a coma, she immediately reached out, took my hand, and said "Oh, you're that nice lady who came and said a prayer for me! And you're wearing that same pretty blouse with the flowers on it that you had on the day you came to visit me." While I was trying to recover myself and say something, because I had indeed been wearing "that same pretty blouse" that very day I prayed for her, Cora added, "And thank you so much for the prayers you said for me, especially for my little grandson, Jason. He and 'Grandma' are so close that I knew he'd be having a hard time with all this!"

So how does a woman in a coma "see" a particular blouse and "hear" a silent prayer? I was working in the ER one afternoon when Gwen and Fred, an elderly man and his wife, were brought in by ambulance from the scene of a dreadful accident. We gathered from the EMTs that the couple had been crossing the street when they were hit by a car. Fred was unconscious but not badly injured; he had sustained injuries that, as far as the medical team could discern, he would recover from quickly. Gwen, however, died within an hour of being admitted to the ER. Shortly after her death, a peculiar thing began happening. Fred, stable and still unconscious, began a rapid decline. The medical team fought furiously to save him, but nothing worked; he died just forty-five minutes after his wife had passed. The medical team was stunned and baffled because they could find no reason for Fred to have died. I had the unenviable task of going to the ER waiting room with the doctor to inform the couple's three adult children and their families that not only had their mother died, but they had lost their father as well.

Naturally, the couple's adult children were very, very sad, but despite their grief, all three of them commented on the fact that their parents had been so in love and so close in life that it was unimaginable how one of them could have continued without the other. "Losing them both at once is dreadful," one of them told me, "but you know, on the other hand, I believe they would have wanted to go together like this. It will give me some semblance of peace at least to know that they're together with each other."

How and why Fred died, following his wife in death, is still a mystery. Did he somehow "know" his wife had died even though he was unconscious? Did he "choose" to follow her? Can we actually "choose" to some extent to live or die? Who knows? I am at peace with not knowing at this point. The dying have taught me that I do not need to know, nor will I know, the specifics about a lot of things that I will encounter while working with them. Some things will always remain unknown in this life and on this plane of existence. Although the temptation for me to question such mysteries always lingers, the dying have taught me that it's simply best to trust the unknown.

Chapter Six

DEALING WITH MYSTERY,
EVIL, AND DARKNESS

A<small>T 2:20 A.M., I WAS STANDING IN THE CORRIDOR</small> of the ICU, waiting for our patient, Mrs. Porter, to die, when Dr. Stevenson came out of her room and approached me to talk.

I had received the first page at 12:10 a.m.—a Code Blue—meaning that Mrs. Porter had gone into cardiac arrest. What was unusual about the code was that the medical team had been called to a recovery unit for fairly routine surgeries. What was even more unusual was that Mrs. Porter was a woman in her mid-forties with no history of heart problems or complicating medical issues.

Dr. Stevenson was the doctor on call and leading the code. He happened to be the husband of a good friend of mine—a very affable, easygoing guy who looked more like a TV doctor than a real-life M.D.; he had handsomely disheveled hair, and was trim and tanned all year, always sporting a wide, easy smile. You wouldn't suspect he had just finished four year's residency training and was now doing an additional three years fellowship to be a cardiologist. We ran into each other frequently at the hospital, and he was always calm and in control in an almost breezy manner that inspired both awe and envy.

With his lead, the medical team stabilized Mrs. Porter quickly, then moved her to the ICU for observation as a precaution. My doctor friend made the requisite phone call to her husband, advising him not to even bother coming into the hospital until morning, since things had been resolved so quickly and neatly.

But half an hour later, Mrs. Porter coded again. As the medical team worked furiously to revive her, I informed the charge nurse that I was contacting the family. Mrs. Porter's husband was speechless at the news that his wife had gone into cardiac arrest a second time, and, upon my urging, he hung up to make the hour-long drive in the middle of the night to our hospital.

Fifteen minutes later, Mrs. Porter coded a third time. Once again, the medical team was able to stabilize her, although it took much longer than the first two attempts. Obviously things were not looking good, and I decided to hang around the unit and wait. My one concern was that Mrs. Porter's husband might not make it to the hospital in time to be with his wife before she coded a fourth or even fifth time and expired. You don't normally code three times in one night and live to tell about it. Yet these are the kind of thoughts we keep to ourselves when we're part of a code team. The medical team's job is to do everything they can to save a patient's life, and that they do—suspending feelings, hunches, and judgments, until saving the patient's life is truly no longer an option. After the third code at 2:20 a.m., Dr. Stevenson came out of Mrs. Porter's room and called me aside.

"Did you contact the patient's family?" he asked me.

"I called her husband during the second code, so he's on his way," I said.

For a few minutes, we both just stood there absorbing this. Then my doctor friend looked at me, and I was startled to see him so visibly upset.

"I . . . I don't think we're going to be able to save her," he said, shaking.

"Yes, I can see that," I told him, putting my hand on his arm.

"I don't understand it. There's no medical reason why this woman should be dying," he said. "I don't understand why we can't get her stabilized."

"You're doing the best you can, and that's all you can do," I said.

"Yes, but it doesn't make any sense. I don't think we're going to be able to save her." He looked at me in agony, and it occurred to me yet again how very seriously doctors take their patients' care, and how each failure to bring their patients back to health takes an incredible toll physically and emotionally. While we both stood, taking in the reality of our patient's dire situation, a fourth code was called, prompting us to return immediately into Mrs. Porter's room.

Ultimately, the medical team was unable to save her, and at 3:10 a.m., I accompanied the doctor to the waiting room of the ICU, where we informed the stunned husband that his forty-four-year-old wife, who had come into our hospital just yesterday for a fairly routine procedure, was now dead.

This was perhaps only the first of many "failures" my doctor friend would face throughout his career, and it pained me to see how very hard he took his inability to save the woman's life. It is something to remember about every doctor you run into: even the most thoughtless, arrogant jerk does not simply call a code to a halt, pronounce a patient's death, and walk away unscathed. There is a cost to everything we do in this life, and the personal costs of trying to save lives for nearly all medical personnel are enormous.

The Reality of Suffering

If only every mystery—every unexpected or unwelcome event we encounter as medical and spiritual caregivers—simply baffled us, or challenged our worldview, or changed how we look at life and death for the better. Then mystery would not be the adversary it sometimes seems in our battles to help and ultimately heal our patients. We do not have to work in the medical field very long to encounter horrible, inexplicable "mystery"—young men in their thirties dying of massive heart attacks, or young women barely out of college dying of breast or ovarian cancer. Babies are born healthy and then simply fail to thrive, dying before our eyes of unknown reasons. People die after routine procedures, for no apparent reason, or suffer disproportionately to what we'd think should be any person's "allowable quota" of hardship on the roulette wheel called life.

There is perhaps no more baffling adversary than an untimely, inexplicable, or an apparently meaningless death. Except for perhaps one thing—evil. I believe evil exists in this world, and the evidence is all around us. Innocent people suffer horrifically every day on this planet, and not just in far-off wars in other countries. Many of these sufferers appear every day in our ERs: women beaten within an inch of their lives, children tortured and abused, men who have been shot for walking on the wrong side of the street. The last example might surprise and perplex you unless you work in one of our urban ERs, where every weekend at least one young man comes in with a bullet in his head from gang-related gunfire.

For most Americans, the most iconic act of evil of our era was perhaps, the events of 9/11. Our national psyche and our individual souls were forever scarred by the images of people like us who went routinely and without a hint of foreboding to work on a beautiful, sunny day in late summer and wound up dead. Some hung from a window of the skyscraper, then jumped to their death, or were burned alive by jet-fueled fires, or were smashed to pieces in the collapsing of our nation's tallest buildings. From the perspective of a member of a medical team, perhaps the most poignant images of that day for me were all the medical personnel standing by, waiting eagerly to help all the injured who were to be rushed from Ground Zero to the surrounding hospitals, but who ultimately never arrived.

Then there is the suffering that very seldom makes the headlines. Tens of thousands of people die each year from cancer and heart disease. There are patients who suffer chronic pain from ailments like Crohn's disease, or from some mysterious cause that the doctors cannot fathom. There are individuals who are slowly paralyzed by Lou Gehrig's disease until they eventually stop breathing or choke to death. And perhaps worse than any physical pain is the mental and spiritual pain that comes from wrestling with suffering, its apparent lack of purpose, and our inability to end it. It is when we are not able to make meaning or sense out of the pain and suffering around us that we are most susceptible to severe depression and even vulnerable to suicide. All we can see around us is an inescapable darkness.

Such mysteries, suffering, and spiritual darkness challenge easy assumptions that the universe is a benign place, or that simply "taking good care of ourselves" or being good, spiritually awakened people will help us avoid cancer, chronic disease, evil and injustice, unbearable pain, or untimely death. In the long run, we as spiritual caregivers find ourselves reaching the conclusion that much of what happens to our patients is out of our hands, and that the good we would wish for them doesn't always come to pass. This realization of our sheer helplessness before the sufferings of our patients and loved ones can often be our single biggest suffering and "adversary"—tempting us to plunge into anger, depression, cynicism, and the sort of caregiver burnout that, robbing us of the joy of living and caring for others, makes us ineffectual healers.

What Adversity Can Offer Us

I will never forget a hospice patient I once had, a tiny, elderly woman dying of cancer. While we were praying together during a home visit, she suddenly pulled back, looked me in the eye, and ordered me to leave immediately, as she could see I was "trying to kill her." Completely stunned, I got up to leave, only to be stopped at the door by the hired caregiver who was frantically begging me not to leave. In tears, she told me that the patient was becoming increasingly erratic and even threatening, and that she was afraid to be left alone with her. When the patient in the other room heard that I had, in fact, not left and that I was instead talking with the caregiver, she became even more hysterical, until finally I had no choice but to leave despite the caregiver's desperate pleas.

Back at the office, I told the director of the hospice what had happened. Badly shaken, humiliated, and deeply hurt, I had a good cry over it. I felt I had completely failed the patient in some manner, as well as the caregiver, although I was hard pressed to know what I had done that had caused the patient to think I'd want to kill her. I was also afraid that this situation might mark the end of my brief career as a hospice chaplain. The hospice director, however, was far more pragmatic in her assessment of the situation, which she seemed to take in stride. She warned me that, for a variety of reasons, many patients become confused or even aggressive as their illnesses progress, and that this probably wouldn't be my last unpleasant encounter with such a patient. The director was equally nonplussed when the following day at morning report she informed me that she had received a call from the patient's family, saying I had upset the patient and requested that I no longer visit. She did add, however, that the caregiver who had begged me not to leave had given her immediate notice and left the home as soon as she was able.

Through this painful encounter, my dying patient actually gave me an unwelcomed but ultimately priceless gift. This encounter made me very sensitive to the fact that, despite our very best intentions or efforts, sometimes things do go horribly wrong in our encounters with our patients and their families. It was a hard lesson to learn, but one that helped me help others who found themselves in baffling and unpleasant scenarios with their dying loved ones. Now, when on occasion I listen to family members tell me about the outlandish accusations their loved ones make, or the very hurtful things the dying can say as their illnesses worsen and their mental clarity is impaired, I can draw on my own painful experience to help lessen their own feelings of pain, guilt, or bewilderment, and perhaps bring them some consolation.

Adversity has a lot to teach us, and it can be an almost perverse kind of mentor or friend, often leading us to a deeper, richer life, or even our life's essential calling. For example, we would never have had extensive cancer research if it hadn't been for the many doctors who stood by helplessly watching their patients die from this disease; and cancer research has, indeed, reduced the number of people every year who receive a cancer prognosis as an unquestioned death sentence. We also have made incredible strides in pain management. Many patients who would have died in agony decades ago, now experience relatively little physical pain, all because medical caregivers were scandalized by the degree of suffering their patients endured and did something about it.

Relieving Suffering: "What Awakened People Do"

Dr. Larry Dossey, famous for his advocacy of the power of the mind in health and the role of spirituality in health care, once said that helping and healing people is "what awakened people do." ("Healing and the Nonlocal Mind," *Alternative Therapies 5*, November 1999.)

I had a patient, Harold, who refused to take his pain medications and, as a result, was experiencing tremendous discomfort as he was dying. When I asked why Harold was choosing not to avail himself of relief, he told me that he was a Christian and believed that if Jesus chose to die without having his suffering relieved, who was he to want relief and comfort greater than what Jesus had accepted. Instead of contradicting Harold, I helped him to take a deeper look at his Christian faith, gently pointing out to him all the times in the Bible when Jesus relieved the sickness and suffering of others, rather than praise, condone, or even augment it! Jesus, like "awakened" people throughout time and in all religious and spiritual traditions, chose to help and heal people.

I then asked Harold what he thought Jesus would want for him in this situation. In response, he began to talk about his great sadness at finding himself dying. Faced with the fact that he had not received healing, Harold was bitterly sad and did not feel "worthy" of pain relief, because he felt he was not "worthy" of healing. In fact, his rejection of pain medication went a step further. He was actually trying to punish God at some unconscious level by not accepting what seemed like a poor second choice that God appeared to be offering him instead of a cure for his disease—that is, some sort of physical relief during his journey towards death.

Death is almost always a frightening and unwelcomed end to our earthly pilgrimage. Nevertheless, once we were able to gently unpack Harold's deep anger and sadness, as well as his hidden motivations for his behavior, he was able to face a sad and mysterious situation over which he had no control, and look at the possibility of accepting pain medication. Harold was able to see that taking pain medication would not be because of any personal or spiritual weakness or because he was not loved or cared for enough to receive a healing. Finally able, at some level, to accept that he was dying, Harold realized that his ambivalence over his situation was normal and understood by the God he claimed to follow. This God would not want him to suffer more than he had to when it was possible to alleviate much of the pain in the time that remained.

Ultimately, Harold did indeed receive healing—but not the healing he had hoped for. Healing had initially meant one thing only—a cure of his cancer. The healing Harold received left him with an uneasy peace and acceptance of his dying, even as he remained sad and ambivalent about it. Harold ultimately accepted the healing he received—a renewed sense of Divine love and mercy—by accepting pain management. His spiritual as well as physical suffering was lessened, and he was able to die a dignified and relatively comfortable death.

Spiritual Care as Accompaniment in Suffering

I know countless individuals who have entered helping careers—doctors, nurses, social workers, justice advocates, aid workers, social entrepreneurs, and spiritual caregivers—because of some personal adversity. In the many interviews I've done of people called to care for the sick and dying, I've found that the vast majority of spiritual caregivers chose their work because of some personal or familial crisis. One woman said she felt compelled to become a hospice chaplain because of the exceptional, tender care her mother received when she was dying, while a chaplain friend of mine entered chaplaincy for precisely the opposite reason—because the spiritual care his dying wife had received was virtually nonexistent at the hospital where she was a patient. Many more individuals spoke to me of witnessing that health care or spiritual care was unfairly distributed or even denied to "people like them"—people of color, or women, or gay individuals, or the disabled. Such adversity and suffering "awakened" in them a sense of vocation and a deep compassion for those who were sick and suffering, and they committed their best intentions and abilities to help others caught in the same situations they had once found themselves. All these caregivers chose to accompany the suffering of others with spiritual care.

Out of the pain and tragedy of 9/11, our country has perhaps gone on to make some questionable foreign policy choices. But that horrific event has also produced many heroic acts and sacrifices, as well as a renewed consciousness of our interconnectedness. I have been repeatedly stunned and humbled by the many "survivors" of 9/11, including family and loved ones of those killed, who have chosen to honor their memories with acts of courage and generosity instead of calls for vengeance.

Then there are those caregivers who dare to walk into the darkness on a daily basis. First-responders who put their lives on the line to save the lives of complete strangers; psychiatric doctors and nurses who deal with individuals who are mentally ill or broken by life's difficulties; social workers and counselors who try to deal with ongoing suffering or dysfunction or look for solutions for those trapped in poverty, homelessness, addiction, or domestic violence; and spiritual caregivers who daily walk with patients and families through what is metaphorically referred to as "the valley of the shadow of death," choosing to be with people in their pain and misery in the difficult places where there are no simple answers.

I recall a colleague of mine, a young seminarian doing a semester of chaplaincy training at my hospital, who was called to see a patient dying from cancer. When my young friend tried to "console" the patient by telling him that he had been given this "cross to bear" because God "loved him," the patient told the seminarian, in no uncertain terms, where he could put his "cross" and his "God." I also remember another chaplain who once told a patient that his terrible physical suffering was God's will for him, and who wound up having the infuriated patient hurl the remains of his lunch tray all over the chaplain's face and outfit before demanding he get out of his room. These patients gave my coworkers the unwelcomed gift of their patent refusal to accept easy answers and hollow platitudes regarding the difficult realities of their suffering. These dying patients offered their spiritual caregivers the gift of an authentic response, which in turn pushed them to consider how to be more authentic and effective in the outreach to the sick and dying.

Spiritual caregiving is not for the faint of heart, but spiritual accompaniment of the sick and dying is also not for those who feel comfortable smugly telling others what is their "cross to bear" or "God's will." Spiritual caregiving is not about easy answers. It is about standing with others on what might well be the very worst day of their lives, without judgment and without turning and running. It's about letting people know that we will accompany them and advocate for them until the bitter end, and then some.

Perhaps one of the greatest gifts I can offer patients and their families is my own experience of having repeatedly faced sickness and death. (This is regardless of the fact that I have not been critically or terminally ill; our patients and families do not expect or demand that of us.) I will never forget a patient's wife who, as her husband lay dying, admitted to me in a panic that she had never watched anyone die before and therefore was terrified about not knowing what to do. I believe that she was unique only to the degree in which she was able to articulate what so many family members actually experience as their loved ones lay dying.

I took her hand and told her that I had been with many people when they were about to die, and that not only would I stay and be with her while her husband died, but I would help her take care of everything that needed to be done after he passed. What patients and families expect and deserve from us is a balance of compassion, honesty, common sense, and concrete help. As caregivers, we can give them some degree of consolation and courage because of our experience. We have walked others down the path to death. And we can commit to take that uncomfortable walk yet again—this time with them. This is what spiritual care giving is all about—accompaniment.

How do we face mystery, evil, and suffering on a regular basis, caring for and accompanying others physically as well as spiritually in times of illness and impending death? How is this kind of accompaniment possible, and from where do we get our strength to balance the personal costs of such accompaniment?

The "Accompaniment" of Those Who Have Passed

I truly believe this kind of accompaniment through mystery, evil, illness, and suffering is only possible with the help of others, and that the strength we need to continue is a strength that can only come from sources beyond our own means. It is my belief that there is a "power" outside of myself that accompanies me in my "accompaniment" of others, giving me and my patients and families the strength that is not of this world. This power is the source of an unlimited love and compassion that I have seen countless times touch and transform those who are suffering. This strength is the source of an unlimited and almost crazy hope, and a renewed sense of purpose that I have seen transform even the most bitter and depressed individuals. Without this power and strength, I would never have lasted very long working as a spiritual caregiver in a medical environment.

Likewise, I have seen patients and families come through the darkness because they have received a tiny glimpse of light—the source of which was beyond their own efforts and resources—which gave them the strength, courage, and consolation to continue in what otherwise appeared to be meaningless suffering. I think it's no mistake that patients often report going toward a bright light during near-death experiences; that light, I believe, is the same special power and strength that touched them in this life and waits to greet them in the next.

Not only do our dying patients and loved ones have much to teach us while they remain on this Earth, but they continue to assist us after they die. You might recall that my husband is from Ireland. So was my grandfather; he immigrated to America as a teenager. My grandfather and my husband's father died many years before Stephen and I met, but it is our strong belief that both of them had a hand in our meeting, despite the fact that for most of our lives neither my husband nor I even lived in the same country. My husband and I often joke that his dad and my grandfather are sitting in some sort of celestial version of an Irish pub, toasting our marital union with a pint of Guinness.

Likewise, I feel very strongly that my departed patients often come to my assistance, helping me give good spiritual care to my current patients. Something a former patient said or did will come into my mind to inspire me to help another patient in a particular manner, and I'll have a curious sense of the former patient's presence and/or approval. I have been fortunate to live a very full and rich life, and I truly believe this, too, has been no accident, but has been possible in part because of the "intercession" of my departed patients and loved ones.

Because my family lived in Asia when I was a teenager, I wound up having many friends from Buddhist, Confucian, and Hindu backgrounds who had home altars devoted to their ancestors. They prayed to them for help and assistance, even offering them incense, little bowls of rice, or tiny goblets of wine to assuage their "hunger" or "thirst." As a young adult, I found these religious traditions a bit off-putting, although I never questioned the mainline Christian notion of the Communion of Saints, which is a belief that our departed loved ones are in another realm, helping us as we, too, can help assuage any spiritual hunger or thirst that might have accompanied them, unresolved, into the next life. Now, the traditions of the Eastern and Western religions regarding our departed loved ones do not look so dissimilar. In fact, I have found that all the world's religions and great spiritual traditions hold remarkably similar teachings in many areas, including the belief that somehow we do not simply cease to exist when we experience physical death. Almost every great religious tradition asserts that in some manner we go on, and most of those traditions also indicate that we can even hope to see our departed loved ones again one day. I find in these beliefs—the results of the accumulated experience and wisdom of our ancestors and their interaction and experience with the Divine—perhaps the most compelling reason to hope, in the face of mystery, evil, and spiritual darkness, that suffering and death do not have the final word.

Chapter Seven

THE HEALING POWER OF HUMOR

A H, THE STORIES I COULD TELL YOU. There was Luke, that very handsome young man who was dead upon arrival from smoke inhalation—his face and physique eerily unblemished, but with a smell of fire so strong that we had to run a fan to dissipate the fumes. The entire staff was mourning over Luke's lost life and lost potential until his fiancées starting arriving at the ER—all four of them—whereupon we shifted our attention to keeping them off one another.

Another time, I had a date at a wine bar in downtown Chicago immediately after my shift, so I dressed in my nicest outfit for my last appointment of the day—a hospice visit with one of our nurses to see an elderly woman in her home. During our visit, our patient suddenly and urgently needed to get to the toilet. As the nurse and I struggled to help her to the commode, it became very apparent that she wasn't wearing a protective undergarment of any sort beneath her house dress, because, without warning, she began defecating all over my best shoes. Laughing so hard she had tears streaming down her cheeks, the nurse informed me that now, after that rather unsavory baptism by fire, I was indeed a *real* chaplain in her book. I showed up for my date in sneakers.

Once, when I was fairly new on the palliative care floor, the nurses neglected to tell me about the elderly man who liked to page the female chaplains to his room, and greet them from a chair by the window . . . buck naked. Nor did they warn me about the other elderly gentleman who feigned being hard of hearing so you'd have to get so close to him you were nearly shouting in his ear, whereupon he grabbed your breasts with much more vigor than you'd ever think a dying old man could muster.

Then there was the time I phoned a patient's wife and before I had a chance to identify myself, she told me she knew exactly who I was, swore at me, calling me every conceivable name in the book—and then some!—and warned me never to call their home again or she'd hunt me down and give me what was coming to me! You can imagine her response when, after her tirade, I cleared my throat and told her I was calling from the ER of the local hospital, wishing to inform her that her husband had just been admitted with minor injuries from a traffic accident.

That incident reminds me of the woman who came into our ER, begging me to see her boyfriend who had sustained injuries in a traffic accident and was waiting in one of the cubicles to go up to X-ray. We let her back to see him, and when we returned three minutes later to take him up to X-ray, we discovered the two of them having some of the most creative sex you can imagine, given the limitations of the hospital gurney, the patient's injuries, and the IV pole he was hooked up to.

These accounts represent but a few anecdotes in a litany of one caregiver's experiences, both humorous and poignant, documenting the small humiliations, misadventures, and foibles of working with the sick and dying. Such interludes are actually welcome bits of respite, offering caregivers a much-needed lift and a different perspective from the predictable and debilitating horrors of illness.

It is standard belief among many medical professionals that laughter and humor are good for the body, as well as the mind and spirit. Recent studies have documented the physical benefits and stress reduction of laughter, and many hospitals consider "laughter therapy" one of the many complementary therapies in a patient's potential "healing regimen." Clown therapy and humor carts, consisting of DVDs featuring situation comedies and funny movies, are common in many medical facilities. Equally important are the unexpected humorous events and exchanges, in the midst of the pain and suffering. They are a grace and a gift, bringing deep healing of the spirit to both patients and caregivers, who are taken by surprise.

Humor is a lot like sex: dying patients and their families still need a fair amount of it, but sometimes they are bothered by a nagging sense of guilt—that it is "inappropriate" in the face of death. We forget that not only can a good laugh produce a wonderful physical and spiritual release, but that humorous events can also provide us with intimate moments, wonderful memories, and great stories to share, long after our patients and loved ones have left us.

"His Name Isn't Bill. It's Peter."

I was called to the Intensive Care Unit to say a prayer with the family of an elderly man who had just died. It was an unusual day in that I was literally running from one death to another; this elderly gentleman was "Patient Number 5" of seven patients who would die on my shift that day. As I arrived to pray with his family, I was very aware that calls to the bedsides of "Patient Number 6" and "Patient Number 7" were probably imminent. (This may sound like a rather crude way of talking about the passing of human beings out of this life, but I want to show how difficult the work of spiritual caregiving can be, and what kind of mental state a caregiver can arrive in, entering a situation requiring great reverence, respect, and compassion.) So, prior to going into the patient's room, I tried to gather myself together at the nursing station, taking the time to review with the nurse the patient's situation.

When I entered the room, two women introduced themselves as the patient's daughters. Tearfully they each held their father's hand and told me how long he had been ill and how he had died so peacefully prior to my arrival. They asked me to say a prayer for their father's "safe journey," whereupon I took a deep breath, quieted myself, then launched into what I thought was my finest chaplain mode, offering what I thought was a good, solemn, and dignified prayer. Halfway through it, however, both daughters, who I thought had been stifling their grief as I prayed, had actually been stifling giggles, and now were laughing uncontrollably, tears rolling down their faces.

When they were able to get control of themselves, one of the daughters said to me, "His name isn't Bill, it's Peter," at which I realized, to my horror, that "Bill" was three patients ago! While I literally stumbled over myself apologizing for my mistake, Peter's daughters once again dissolved into fits of hysteria, finally catching their breaths long enough to warmly and graciously absolve me of any guilt or wrongdoing. One of the daughters later told me that neither of them could really say why they found my mistake so funny, except that their father, an inveterate prankster, had had a rather mischievous sense of humor and would most likely have had a good laugh over my flawed eulogy.

"I know you think we should have been upset hearing our dad called some other name at a time like this, but it was like we got to have one last, unexpected laugh with him," the daughter told me. "It was like he was trying to say to us, 'Don't be too sad, now. We'll all be together having ourselves a laugh or two before you know it.' Frankly, I couldn't have thought of a better way to send Dad off."

Often, many patients display a remarkable capacity for humor even as they are dying. Remember my two little old men on the palliative care unit? It is as if the patients need relief from the constant stress of dealing with their own imminent mortality, finding such relief in something as simple as playing a practical joke on their caregivers. Not only do pranks inject a bit of humor into mundane or even intimidating scenarios, but they help the patient feel and maintain a sense of control in situations where the medical staff appears to hold all the power.

Back in my early days of chaplaincy, I had a patient named Bobbie, a drag queen who was dying of AIDS. Remarkably, right up to the time of his death, Bobbie managed a full face of make-up, elaborate wigs, and a coy, fetching, and flirtatious demeanor—especially around and to the discomfort of our male staff—that belied the fact that he was dying slowly and painfully from a variety of grisly ailments. Bobbie even managed to maintain long, polished and manicured nails that put my own to shame, and he had a dry, almost cutting wit about him. When I visited him, he appraised my wardrobe, usually drolly, giving me hints on improving my appearance. "You'll never hook a man with that unibrow, Deary," he told me. Bobbie often complained about having to wear the hospital gown, saying he couldn't abide the fact that he was going to die swathed in such a dismal color. While most of the staff assisted Bobbie in maintaining his appearance as well as his sense of humor, a few staff members thought that it was my duty as chaplain to help him "become himself" (rather than "herself") and squarely face the fact that he was dying.

I disagreed. I believed Bobbie was indeed himself—or herself—to such a degree that, even while dying, Bobbie fought to maintain his dignity and appearance, a struggle that didn't necessarily mean he was refusing to face the fact that he was dying. I was sometimes saddened, though, that Bobbie's consistently rakish humor created an atmosphere where it was difficult to talk seriously about anything. Still, this was his choice—to die as he had lived, and I needed to honor that choice.

Despite his need to maintain a sense of distance and control, Bobbie was a deeply spiritual man, and we always ended our visits with a prayer, often led by him. In the end, I wound up sitting with him, the same way as I do with so many patients; I sat, holding his hand and praying for him, at his request, until he breathed his last breath.

Solidarity and Humility in Moments of Humor

Like many speakers of a second or third language, my ability to communicate in a language that is not my "mother tongue" diminishes proportionate to my stress. I have had many Latino patients, some of whom are very recent immigrants to this country, so I've often resorted to communicating in Spanish. I can communicate basic ideas and am culturally competent enough to give relatively appropriate and culturally sensitive care, but I make an awful lot of mistakes. Luckily most of my Latino patients, like Peter's daughters, are big-hearted and forgiving.

Once, I was dealing with Dolores, a woman whose husband had been shot while they were refueling at a gas station. Recent immigrants, they did not realize that the husband had inadvertently been wearing "gang colors," and that he was shot by rival gang members for intruding in what was perceived to be their territory. Even though the man had been shot in the face at fairly close range, remarkably, he was not badly injured and was going to survive. Understandably emotional, Dolores was making a bit of a scene in our ER waiting area, so I was called to calm her down. Speaking Spanish, I thought I was repeatedly inviting her to calm down and sit down, to which she responded with an explosion of laughter to the point of tears. I later realized that I had been telling Dolores to calm down and "feel herself!" Later she thanked me, telling me that this humorous episode had snapped her out of an uncontrollable sense of panic, which allowed her to recover her inner resources and realize she could get through this horrible event.

Another time I was assisting a Latino family with finding a priest to anoint their dying aunt. The family's priest lived more than an hour away, so they were afraid he would not make it to the hospital in time to be with their aunt before she died. Even though we did not have a priest on staff, I assured the family not to worry, that our staff had a good relationship with a local priest who could come to the hospital to anoint their aunt as a favor for us. While I thought I was explaining that the staff had a "good relationship" with the priest, what I had wound up saying was that the staff was having sex with the priest, and that as a reciprocal favor he'd come and anoint their aunt! After the young English-speaking son pointed out the faux pas and everyone stopped laughing, I realized the whole dynamic of the situation had shifted from a somber, edgy, and emotionally distant interaction—between a family of immigrants and an unknown and perhaps unwelcomed member of the majority culture—to a working relationship filled with warmth, good humor, and trust. Ironically, because of my poor Spanish, I was able to aid this family in a manner that might not have been possible were I more linguistically adept, and consequently a little too "professional" and intimidating.

I have learned, perhaps the hard way, that if I am able to have enough humility to admit that I am mistaken or simply lacking in my abilities, then my patients and families are usually willing to accept my limitations and forgive my faults. And when I am willing to laugh at myself or let the joke be on me, it can potentially open a "graced moment" for others, providing relief from the hard realities of death and dying. You can neither "buy" these moments, nor plan or manufacture them. They are graced moments, to be accepted as they present themselves. It is the spiritual caregiver's task to recognize and honor that which is grace and gift and to give that grace and gift "center stage" when its appearance is for the good of those in our care.

Humor at the Very Worst Moment . . . or Not?

In a hospital setting, humor can border on the macabre, yet what at first seems horrifying can be ultimately honored, welcomed, and sometimes even prove profoundly healing. I arrived at the ICU where my patient, Mr. Lane, was actively dying, only to be introduced to two Mrs. Lanes! Because the women seemed disinclined to offer me any assistance as to which of the two was the man's wife, I snuck out of the room to talk to the nurse, who informed me that the tinier of the two women was Mr. Lane's first wife, and the rather heavy woman his current wife. I returned to the room, steeling myself for what I thought was the inevitable, uncomfortable confrontation between the two women, but it never materialized. Each wife appeared to accept the presence of the other, although their demeanor toward one another was distant and frosty. The former Mrs. Lane was resigned to the fact that Mr. Lane was dying, while Mr. Lane's current wife was nearly hysterical, squeezing the patient's hand and begging him to live, imploring me to pray for a miracle.

I never like to give people false hope, and I could see that Mr. Lane's vital signs were steadily dropping toward "flatline," at which moment he would be declared dead. However, despite all our technology and advanced learning, none of us truly knows exactly when somebody will die, even when death looks imminent. It is one of the mysteries of life that death will come when it does, and not when or if we're ready for it, or even when trained medical professionals say it will come. Also, it is my duty as a spiritual caregiver to honor the requests of my patients and their loved ones to the extent to which those requests are not harmful. If a person wants to pray for a miracle, it is not my place to tell them that I don't think this looks like a good time for a miracle. Our patients' healing, just like their deaths, is not something we can control. So, I did offer a prayer for Mr. Lane's recovery, but I also snuck in a request for the grace to accept that that recovery might not be forthcoming and that Mr. Lane's loved ones receive strength and consolation during this difficult transition.

Right at that very moment, the life support monitor flatlined, and the alarms went off to indicate that Mr. Lane had died. The current Mrs. Lane began screaming over the alarm, "Live, live, live!" For a moment it appeared as if Mr. Lane was going to accommodate her. Several moments after being declared dead, Mr. Lane heaved what looked like an enormous sigh and promptly fell over in bed, whereupon the current Mrs. Lane screamed "He's alive, he's alive!" then fainted dead away right on top of me.

Sometimes during death, as in the case of Mr. Lane, the muscles contract in a manner that causes movement—for example, an exhalation of gases built up can give the very eerie and unsettling appearance that a dead person is indeed alive and breathing. In reality, it is only a physical response of the body shutting down. I was doing a rather poor job—from a rather undignified vantage point—of explaining this to the former Mrs. Lane, as she and the nurse and two nurses' aides, all stifling their laughter, tried to lift the current and sizeable Mrs. Lane off my prone body. While they eased the patient's wife into a chair and tried to revive her, I tried to recover myself. But after four people have had to lift one of your patient's loved ones off your sore, flattened, and somewhat wrinkled being, the chances of being taken seriously are diminished. At a moment when I should have been giving comfort to the patient's loved ones, his former wife was soothing me, insisting I "sit a spell" and asking *me* if *I* needed to see a doctor!

However, this unlikely turn of events provided just the sort of healing these two wives needed. As the current Mrs. Lane was coming to, the former Mrs. Lane clucked her tongue and almost playfully chided her, saying, "Now, Lunetta, why'd you have to go and make such a scene of yourself like that?" whereupon the current Mrs. Lane looked up at her and broke into tears. "I just wanted him to live, so badly," she cried. The former Mrs. Lane softened visibly and cooed, "Me too, baby, me too," and embraced the other woman. The two cried with each other—tears of relief. And an hour later, both women left the ICU together, hugging me fondly, pinching my arms to make sure they were still working and chuckling over my small misfortune. They told me what a good chaplain I had been to them, then walked arm-in-arm out of the hospital.

In all honesty, I know that I had very little to do with what unfolded that afternoon, other than my role as victim in a macabre situation that served to break the terrible tension between two estranged women facing their husband's death. It was humor that broke the icy expanse separating these two grieving women. It was humor that catalyzed these women to exchange what only they could give one another—comfort, support, healing, and even forgiveness.

Chapter Eight

THE JOURNEY FROM
DENIAL TO ACCEPTANCE

THE HOSPICE SECRETARY INTERRUPTED the morning staff meeting to give one of the nurses an urgent message. Mrs. Romano wanted the nurse to come out to her home immediately, the secretary told me, quoting the phone message, "because something had changed in her husband's condition." The nurse nodded and, leaning across the table, said to me, "I think you better join me on this one, Chaplain."

"Any particular reason?" I asked, not relishing seeing Mrs. Romano again. On my initial visit, Mrs. Romano had told me, point-blank, that I shouldn't waste my time coming out to see her again. She was one of those fiercely independent, old-fashioned, Italian-American women I am so very familiar with because of my own Italian-American roots—direct, somewhat suspicious of strangers, and priding herself on caring for her home and family. Talking with a chaplain was a touchy-feely waste of time as far as she was concerned.

"I think you better join me on this one, because Mrs. Romano might need a chaplain after all. I'd bet my right arm her husband is probably dead."

"Dead? But the secretary quoted her as saying something had changed with her husband's condition." Surely "dead" is a condition Mrs. Romano would have noticed, and one that needed relatively little diagnosis or explanation from the nurse. The nurse rolled her eyes and looked at me like she was dealing with a child.

"Come on," she said, pushing her chair away from the table. "You'll see, and maybe you'll learn something on this trip about the kind of denial our patients and their families can be dealing with when it comes to death."

When we arrived at the Romano home, sure enough we discovered that Mr. Romano had passed away during the night. The nurse checked his vitals and confirmed his status, while Mrs. Romano remained some distance away.

"Yes," she admitted to us hesitantly, as if she almost didn't believe it herself. "I thought something was different about him this morning."

Denial

Years ago, Dr. Elisabeth Kübler-Ross identified five stages in the dying process that have become classic guidelines for spiritual caregiving: denial of the situation at hand, bargaining with "the higher powers," becoming angry, slipping into depression, and coming to some form of acceptance. The dying often go back and forth between these stages, but it's important to remember that so do the living.

When people learn that a loved one is dying, many also respond by denying that this could be possible. This denial often takes the form of consulting other medical professionals for a different prognosis, pursuing alternative remedies or therapies, praying for a miracle (also a part of the bargaining stage), or simply flat out denying that their loved one is going to die.

As a chaplain, I have encountered all of these situations numerous times. I have seen patients go from one doctor to another, right up until the moment of death. In fact, in one particularly poignant situation, our hospice program received a new patient who literally died on the elevator ride up from the medical care-floor, where he had been receiving aggressive treatment to battle the cancer. The patient was in our hospice program for all of three minutes. Someone, whether it was the patient, the family, or even the doctor, was not able to admit that he was dying until the patient was moments from death.

I have also encountered many individuals from various religious and spiritual persuasions who have held out—or insisted that they would receive a miracle—right up until the moment of death. In fact, one of the most frustrating situations any caregiver will ever face is when a patient's pastor comes on to the scene, insisting that there will be a miracle cure, if only the family believes hard enough and prays hard enough. These pastors tend to alienate the family from most of the hospital staff by asserting that the staff—including the hospital chaplain—lack sufficient faith to save the dying individual, thus suggesting that the patient and family need to distance themselves from these "unbelievers" and their "negativity" as much as possible.

What almost always happens is that despite prayers and despite belief, the patient dies, and the befuddled pastor makes a hasty exit, leaving the family alone to deal with horrendous grief compounded by guilt that somehow or in some way they just weren't "good enough" for the promised, life-saving miracle.

I have even encountered patients, just days and hours before dying, who asserted that they were not dying but simply ill and that their full and complete recovery or remission was imminent.

Barbara, a middle-aged pastor of a small, independent church, had had breast cancer fourteen years earlier, from which she was "cured." Actually, Barbara's cancer went into remission, but whether you want to call it "remission" or a "miracle" is really not something I want to argue; whenever a patient gets an unexpected life extension, it is something to celebrate. Life is precious, and in most circumstances most people prefer living over dying—a preference I happen to support wholeheartedly. Still, even as it became abundantly clear that this time there would be no remission for her, Barbara refused to believe that she was dying, telling me to stop visiting her if I didn't "believe in miracles" and refusing any sort of palliative care to such an extent that Barbara eventually withdrew from our hospice program, only to die days later.

I was called to one particularly sad and painful situation that involved a family recently emigrated from Eastern Europe. Their teenage son, Marek, was dying from cancer in a particularly dreadful manner. His condition was not the result of a lack of effort on the part the medical staff. In fact, the staff was outraged and distraught because Marek's mother had denied him any of the pain medications normally made available. She believed that the drugs would kill him rather than palliate his pain. Marek, probably for a whole variety of reasons, consented to his mother's assessment of the situation and had gone along with refusing his pain meds, which resulted in him dying a particularly agonizing death. Throughout all this, his mother sat at his bedside and, while begging him not to give up, tried to feed Marek spoonful after spoonful of honey. She believed the honey had curative powers, but her son could ingest very little of it. All the while, the medical staff agonized over their inability to intercede and make the young man's passing more peaceful and pain-free.

It is actually not uncommon for immigrants to be baffled by and suspicious of many of the claims and practices of Western allopathic medicine, as understood and practiced by those of us in the dominant culture of the United States. Yet, it is particularly sad when this understanding chasm cannot be culturally or medically traversed, resulting in a patient and loved ones languishing until death comes.

I believe it is the duty of any spiritual caregiver to move through the stage of denial with the patient and loved ones in a highly compassionate and patient manner, without pushing people to "face reality" more quickly than they are actually prepared to do. My patients have shown me that some terminally ill patients do receive a "reprieve" from their death sentences, whether you want to call it "remission" or "miracle." To pretend that as medical professionals we can tell anyone with certainty when they're going to die is as cruel and dishonest as promising, with no equivocation, that a miracle will happen.

Another important point I have learned from the dying is that most of us can only absorb the shocking news of our loved one's death or our own imminent departure from this world in very small bits and pieces. Once I was called to give spiritual support to a woman whose husband had just died. We said some prayers together, reminisced about her husband's life, and finally began the paper work that accompanies every death in a hospital setting. After completing these tasks, I turned to the woman and, before leaving, asked her,

"Is there anything else I can do for you?" whereupon she asked me, "Yes, can you tell me when you think he might wake up?"

To push an individual to accept a terminal prognosis too quickly or without great compassion and sensitivity can, I believe, actually kill them. I was once in a patient's room when the doctor came in to inform him, without any preamble, that he had Stage 4 pancreatic cancer, which is "always terminal" and for which there is no cure. After telling the patient that he had only two weeks to live, the doctor turned and walked out of the room! The patient went into a state of severe shock from which he never emerged and he died within twenty-four hours.

Bargaining: Moving In and Out of Denial and Acceptance

When people begin moving out of denial toward a degree of acceptance of dying, it is not at all uncommon to "backslide." During such moments, denial resurfaces and asserts itself. A patient may experience a surging of energy or a lessening of particular symptoms due to medical treatment, often triggering a rise in their hope of getting better.

On any given day or in any given situation, a patient may experience several of these stages all at once. This is what I believe was happening to my patient (see Chapter 6) who was refusing pain medication ostensibly because of his religious beliefs. While it appeared that the patient had *accepted* his death and even went so far as to accept a death filled with physical suffering similar to and in solidarity with the death of the founder of his belief system, the patient was actually *angry* with God for failing to cure his cancer. He reasoned that God was punishing him. I believe this is a type of *bargaining* at a very real and elemental level, not unlike throwing a tantrum in order to get your way. The patient was also in a severe depression that blocked his ability to see the situation in any other manner or to accept what help might have been at hand to ease his suffering.

When patients have, to some extent, accepted that they are dying, it is not at all uncommon for them to believe that they are dying because of something they did or didn't do, and they turn to "the higher power" of this

universe—whether that be God, or the laws of karma, or even their doctor—
in an effort to strike a bargain. One of my patients believed she was dying
because she hated her mother-in-law so much, and she had hoped if she
promised to be nicer to her mother-in-law in the future, maybe she would be
cured. Many patients have come to the unhappy conclusion that they lived
lives that were less than generous; they've asked me to pray for a cure for their
disease, promising me that they will reform if an extension is granted to their
lives. It is indeed sad and sobering to be dying and feel as if life was not lived
as fully and generously as possible.

This harkens back to Chapter 1 on the subject of risk and regret. Regret is a
prominent part of the bargaining stage, as well as the stages of anger and depression. Yet, I don't think regret necessarily haunts only those we imagine have lived
outrageously selfish lives. All of us "fall short" of having lived our lives as kindly,
generously, and as fully as we could have, and all of us will face regrets when we
are dying. For that very reason, the bargaining stage can bring about great riches
in our personal and spiritual life; even in the short time we have left, we can face
some of our regrets and take action concerning some of our unlived dreams or
unfulfilled tasks. We can realize that we have hurt others and apologize to them.
We can see that we have behaved in a manner that was not helpful to ourselves
and others and choose to put those behaviors aside, even if all we have left are a
few weeks or months to live.

My dying patients have taught me much about the wisdom in living in the
moment. In fact, many of my dying patients have expressed a changed relationship with time as they once knew it. Often, time seems to stand still or unfold
in a rich, deep, and focused manner that the dying seldom experienced prior to
their terminal prognosis. Many patients have told me about powerful, liminal
experiences they have had, or moments of intense clarity or richness that had
an eternal quality despite being rooted in the present moment.

Anger

When we were young and growing up, many of us received the message
that anger is bad, and that when we are angry we are bad people. Although

this sounds like a simple, childish concept that most of us have outgrown, much of what we were taught as children remains buried deep within us. My experience with the dying has taught me that many people have great difficulty expressing anger in a manner that is helpful to their ultimate inner healing.

My patient Diane simply refused to get angry, to the point that she was ready to explode from suppressing her rage. You could read it in the lines of her face and hear it in the sharp edge of her voice, despite her stalwart attempts to be smiling and upbeat. Diane dutifully asked me to come by to pray with her, but she kept a tight grip on what prayers to say and how we were going to say them. She had a need to always appear religiously pious and in control of herself, behaviors that I could see were not serving her as she became more and more ill. Finally, we had a conversation in which I invited her to consider that most people in her situation would be very angry. Diane flatly denied that she was the least bit angry, but once the subject had been broached, there was no turning back. Eventually she exploded into a fit of rage, screaming and sobbing uncontrollably for nearly forty-five minutes; then she stopped and became unresponsive for several hours.

While my gut told me that this was precisely what the patient needed, the resulting calamity had me second-guessing my instincts. However, Diane was a changed woman the next time I visited her. She told me that after her crying fit, a horrible sadness at finding herself dying had overwhelmed her, during which she also felt strangely calm at a deep and mysterious level. As time passed, she experienced less and less sadness and more and more calm. The ability to at last express her anger about dying opened up a more authentic manner in which to face death, and brought about tranquility and acceptance—something that previously had eluded her. In a relatively short time, this patient had passed through all five stages of dying.

Diane still experienced moments of deep sadness, but now she was also able to see what a rich life she had been privileged to live. "I am not happy to be dying," she told me, "but I have a sense that I can get through this and that it will be OK." For some of us the words "I can get through this" may appear strange, meaning "I will die." Or "It will be OK" may appear to mean "I'm going to be dead." Yet, the dying have shown me that in coming to terms with their dying, they receive a deep sense of peace and an inexplicable hope that literally carries them through to their deaths.

I have been shown that anger is something to be faced and embraced, for it is a liberating gift leading to honesty, authenticity, acceptance, even grief. It is only in squarely facing our own inner fears and demons that we can transition toward deep joy and peace, even in the midst of dying.

Depression

Depression is perhaps the hardest stage for loved ones and caregivers to witness and deal with. Loved ones and caregivers can feel extremely helpless to alleviate a sick person's suffering; they may feel alienated by the sick person's depression at precisely the point that time appears to be running out. Depression is also one of the hardest and most frightening places for patients, and one of the reasons why they put so much effort into maintaining the stages of denial and bargaining for as long as possible. The worst possible scenario is when patients never emerge from their depression.

Sheila, a woman in her early forties, came into our hospital with a very advanced stage of cancer. Her diagnosis took her totally by surprise, and Sheila immediately withdrew and became unresponsive to the medical team. She was discharged, but several weeks later she was brought back to our hospital, where, to the great shock and horror of her family members who knew nothing about her cancer, she died.

Another poignant lesson I have learned is that depression is a difficult but necessary step in the journey toward an acceptance of dying. Grieving the end of life is a very important step in ultimately letting life go. However, my patients have also taught me that as a caregiver I need to be vigilant in terms of discerning whether the depression they find themselves in is a brutal but important step to another level or a trap from which they cannot escape. Sometimes medical and psychological interventions are needed in cases of extreme, unresolved depression. Other times, the intervention necessary is not of this world.

You might remember Amadou, the hospice patient from Ghana who was extremely depressed and withdrawn until he saw an angel, dressed like the women of his native country, appearing to him and giving him a message of comfort. You might also recall the story about Tom, the gentleman who was admitted to our hospice unit in such terror of dying that the staff despaired of being able to alleviate his inner suffering . . . until his own angel appeared to him and promised to "take him home" with her. Sometimes, the most effective "treatment" for the extreme sadness and terror that can plague a dying patient is a "treatment" above and beyond human understanding, invention, or intervention; the mysterious and loving intercession and insight that come to the patient from outside of themselves usually arrives in an unexpected manner and is often unsought or unbidden, but always tailor-made to fit that particular patient's situation and needs.

In Chapter 4 we discussed "nearing death awareness," a state in which the patient begins to interact with a world which their loved ones and caregivers cannot see or hear. Most of my patients who experienced this phenomenon were hovering back and forth between the stages of depression and acceptance. The nearing death awareness experience often helps to give patients a gentle nudge from fear and depression into a place of acceptance and peace.

A Place of Acceptance and Peace

A dying person may have a near-death experience prior to death as a result of a medical intervention—an experience that can impel a letting go of some of the sadness and fear around dying. One such case involved Ryan, a young man— only nineteen—with advanced terminal cancer and his family members who were fighting to keep him alive at all costs. The family insisted that, were Ryan's heart or breathing to stop, all measures should be taken by the medical staff to revive him, even though reviving him would extend not only his life but his extreme suffering. Ryan did indeed code, and the code team was called in and they revived him, but what happened next was truly astounding. Right after being stabilized, Ryan woke up and, after days of having been too weak to speak, very clearly told his family that he did not want to be revived again; he wanted to be let to die in peace. It is important to understand that when people are resuscitated through CPR, they don't just simply wake up to have a conversation with people shortly afterwards. This young man told his family that he had seen where he was going and that he wanted to go there. He did not want to be held back any longer. At first the family grieved and resisted somewhat, but soon they were able to reach the point where they assured Ryan that they would respect his wishes. In the end, they asked the medical team to change the young man's code status to "DNR" or "Do Not Resuscitate." Almost immediately Ryan slipped back into a coma and died.

While the dying often receive extraordinary assistance on the road to acceptance and inner healing, they have shown me the power and importance of caregivers' ordinary acts of kindness, as well as loving attention to even the least of a patient's expressed needs.

"Granny Mae," as she liked to be called, was a tiny woman from a rural "holler" in backwoods Appalachia who was dying at the residential hospice in North Carolina where I was interning. One morning I came in to find Granny Mae sobbing disconsolately in bed. So I sat with her, holding her hand, until she spent herself crying, and then I observed by way of conversation that she was having a very difficult morning.

"It's this dying business," Granny Mae said with a sniff and a deep sigh. "It's just robbed me of everything!"

"I bet that's got to feel really rotten," I said. "Tell me, what is it you feel most robbed of, Granny Mae?"

"Oh, taking care of people. That's been my whole purpose in life ever since I was fourteen and had my first young'un. I raised eight children and then helped them raise twenty-one grandchildren. Then I even took care of some of my great-grandchildren. I just love young'uns, but now there's nobody I can take care of. Instead you all have to take care of me! I may as well just die and get it over with—I'm useless like this!"

While Granny Mae was speaking, one of our nursing assistants—a local boy barely out of high school—came into the room and immediately joined in the conversation.

"You're not useless, Granny Mae. You rule!" he told her passionately, to which Granny Mae scrunched up her wizened face and asked, "I rule? Like a queen or something?"

I was about to explain the popular expression "you rule," which apparently she wasn't familiar with despite all her years with young'uns, but fortunately and providentially the nursing assistant beat me to the punch.

"Yeah, Granny Mae, you got it. You rule, just like a queen. You're queen around here, you know that?"

"I'm queen?" she asked, now smiling despite herself. And that's how Granny Mae quite literally became "Queen of the Hospice." Word quickly spread of Granny's Mae's amusement at the idea of being a queen. Soon she was officially "crowned" with a foil-paper tiara, no less, which meant that we, her "subjects," would wait on her hand and foot—after all, that's the treatment a queen is bestowed—and that, as queen, she would receive the "homage" of her "loyal subjects" because that's what a queen is accorded.

It was just such a subtle shift in perception, along with some creative role playing, that allowed Granny Mae to accept and enjoy her remaining days, not as someone who perceived herself as "useless" and a burden, but as a regal and queenly woman whose "loyal subjects" loved and adored her enough to serve her meals in bed, take her out to the garden in her wheelchair, and tuck her tenderly into bed for her frequent naps. Which begs the question: Wouldn't it be something if instead of treating our depressed and broken-hearted patients and elderly like problems needing to be taken care of or fixed, we actually treated them like kings and queens?

Sarah Jane, another elderly patient in our residential hospice, was terribly depressed and cried frequently. When she started refusing to see her loved ones, the nurse and I sat down to determine if there was anything we could do to help her. What we found out was that she was terribly upset over how she looked—bloated from her medications and "unpresentable" without access to her make-up or weekly hair appointment at the beauty salon. Without any means to make herself more presentable, she felt too ashamed to see anyone. We received permission from the hospice supervisor to call Millie, a retired hair dresser who worked with our oncology department. Millie helped women who had lost their hair from chemotherapy learn how to improve their appearance with scarves and wigs and to manage their hair as it began growing back. Millie not only washed and set Sarah Jane's hair but gave her a full face of make-up and a manicure, all while chatting as if they were having a regular appointment at the beauty salon. On top of this, Millie gave Sarah Jane her "business card" so Sarah Jane could call her up any time she needed another complimentary hair appointment. Just this simple "beauty treatment" and the kindness of a stranger-turned-loyal-bedside-beautician radically improved the emotional state of our patient, who then began accepting visitors and remained relatively upbeat and serene right until the end.

What exactly does "acceptance" look like when what is being "accepted" is the fact that we're dying—not at some vague and mythic point in the distant future, but now, within weeks, days, or hours? I don't think "acceptance" ever means we reach some sublime inner state where all that's left to do is lie back in our hospital beds to serenely wait for death to come and claim us. Acceptance can be filled with moments of deep sadness as well as episodes of inexplicable joy and gratitude. Acceptance can feel strong one day and weak the next. Acceptance still acknowledges that there are questions that may go unanswered on this side of the grave, or life-long dreams that will never be realized. Acceptance means facing the fact that our loved ones and family members may disappoint us in our final days, or that a longing for reconciliation might not come about. But most of all, acceptance is not "giving up." Acceptance is embracing the time remaining to us and trying to live it out as purposefully, meaningfully, consciously, and fully as our physical limitations allow, bouts of fear, inner pain, and disappointment notwithstanding.

Mystic and spiritual guide Wayne Teasdale was a "lay monk"—an individual who took monastic vows but lived out in the world rather than in a monastery. Teasdale devoted several hours of each day to meditation, contemplation, and spiritual readings, taught spirituality at various colleges, participated in interfaith dialogue around the globe, and was friends with many of the great spiritual thinkers of our era, including the Dalai Lama, Bede Griffiths, Fr. Thomas Keating, and Ken Wilbur. Yet when Teasdale got cancer, he found himself struggling with many of the same feelings most people experience when they are diagnosed: fear, nagging worry, loneliness, and an intense feeling of isolation. He documents his struggles with cancer, as well as the gift that he believes struggling with cancer brought him, in his book, *A Monk in the World.* I mention Wayne Teasdale and his story because I think it is very important for people to realize that even for the "saints" among us (those who devote their lives to higher causes and spend much of their lives in spiritual practice), wrestling with powerful, raw fears and emotions around a terminal prognosis is part of the necessary process of accepting our mortality. Certainly Teasdale's life of prayer, spiritual quest, and monastic practice was of assistance to him as he was dying. But he still had to go through the process. It is a *process* to come to some sense of peace and acceptance of our impending death, and it is a process that will look different for each person going through it. I believe Teasdale ultimately came to a sense of peace about his prognosis and his dying; he was able to learn from his cancer and to value the riches of his journey through cancer. I have learned that individuals who have spent significant time engaged in spiritual search and practice—whether they have embraced a particular faith tradition, spiritual path or practice, or are independent, honest seekers in their own right—usually have an easier time moving through the stages of dying and coming to a place of peace.

Where does the grace to accept death come from? I called the acceptance of death a "grace" because I believe acceptance of this magnitude is indeed a *grace*—aid given to the dying person by a higher power from a higher plane of existence or inner awareness.

The grace to accept our imminent death can come in realizing that we will be survived by the good things we've created, like my patient Lois, busily crocheting her five legacy afghans for each of her grandchildren. The grace to face death can come to us with whiskers and paws, like Nibbles, Miss Hurley's beloved cat, or it can come in the form of an angel to console and carry home a terrified patient. The acceptance of our mortality comes to each of us in a manner unique to our life's journey and unique to our individual needs. I have seen a unique acceptance and peace in each of my patients who dared to ultimately face their own imminent mortality. In doing so, they gave me the gift of knowing that in the final moments on Earth we can and will receive help greater than our own immediate resources.

Chapter Nine

FORGIVENESS

M RS. JACKSON HAD BEEN TAKING CARE OF HER HUSBAND in their home around the clock, seven days a week, 365 days a year, ever since he had been immobilized by a massive stroke seven years earlier. Except for a nursing aide, who sat with Mr. Jackson nights while his wife slept, and the occasional assistance from family members and our hospital's respite care program, Mrs. Jackson monitored her husband's feeding and hydration, turned him every two hours to prevent bed sores, and changed his diapers and sheets several times a day, every day of the week. An African American in her sixties, Mrs. Jackson had come to Chicago from the South nearly forty years ago, yet still spoke in a slow, lilting, and deliberate manner full of poetic turns of speech.

As the Jackson's visiting chaplain, I was astonished by Mrs. Jackson's attention and dedication to her husband and her ability to tend to his all-consuming needs tirelessly and almost single-handedly over many years. Yet, when I praised Mrs. Jackson for her heroic efforts, she just barked out a short laugh and said, "Honey, in many ways these have been the best years of our life together." Then she stared dully at her husband. "At least now I know where he is every night."

I had often wondered what it was that kept Mrs. Jackson going all those years. Was it love or perhaps just spite? Or maybe an ambivalent but not unusual combination of the two that I'm sure often winds up being the underlying emotional current of many long-term relationships. Over a cup of coffee and out of earshot of her husband, I asked Mrs. Jackson if she had forgiven him for his many infidelities throughout their marriage.

"Oh baby, I forgave him for all that long ago," she said with a sigh. "And I have to keep on forgiving him every morning when I get up and go in to see him for the first time that day. It's not as though the idea of some sort of little revenge hadn't occurred to me every now and then, but with God as my witness I never have laid a hand on him, except in love and healing. It's almost like, in the next instance, I see him in a different light for the man he was when he was at his best and while I still loved him with that kind of love you only have when you're young and naïve about all the heartache that life can dish out. But this . . ." she said, fixing her eyes on me suddenly and purposefully, ". . . this is what you get when you get married. It's for better or for worse, baby. Don't you ever forget that. But even the worst . . ." she said with a sigh again, softening, her eyes, her voice trailing off, ". . . even the worst is fertile ground for mercy . . ."

"Fertile ground for mercy." I have turned that phrase over again and again in my mind, regretting that at the time I did not have the courage to ask Mrs. Jackson to elaborate upon her musings. Watching her drift off into her own thoughts, it had seemed invasive to ask for any type of clarification. Yet, something about those words struck me. The words seemed to hint at something important that I was meant to learn about forgiveness and the role forgiveness plays in our relationships. When we experience the worst of those we love or the worst that life can dish out, how is *that* fertile ground, and for what *kind* of mercy? Is it mercy for those who have hurt us? Is it first and foremost mercy and consequently care of and protection for ourselves? Or is it somehow both? And if so, where does that mercy come from? And where, we might also ask, does it take us?

I have thought about that afternoon coffee break with Mrs. Jackson many times throughout the years, especially when I encountered patients and families dealing with issues of forgiveness—or the lack thereof. I have witnessed families and individuals who have refused to extend "mercy" right up to the bitter end and beyond. I have witnessed what to me seemed like atrocious pettiness and cruelty traded back and forth with frightening rancor.

Offering, Withholding, and Forgiveness

I remember two sisters, Nancy and Regina, who refused to talk to one another, although Nancy showed up at the bedside of Regina to faithfully monitor her medical reports—she told me this was her "familial duty." Nancy performed her "duty" in icy silence and without a single word to her sister as she lay there in the hospital bed. When I confronted both of them about their behavior, I learned their mutual rancor revolved around a dining room set!

"I was supposed to get that dining room set when Mother died, and Regina snuck over to the house and took it before I could get there," Nancy told me, livid as if the affront had happened just yesterday even though the "dining room table event"—I would later learn—had happened twenty years ago.

All the while, her sister lay in the bed, gloating, until she finally snapped back, "Well, Nancy, I don't know what you're complaining about. The way things are going here, looks like you're going to get that dining room set after all, now doesn't it?"

I have watched families fracture into feuding parties, blaming one another for everything from who was—or wasn't—taking responsibility for various elements of the patient's care to who the patient loved—or didn't love—more, all while the patient lay within earshot! I can even recall a couple of cases where our medical team had to intervene because family members, who now had power of attorney over helpless patients, were trying to make choices for that patient that would increase rather than decrease their suffering; it wasn't out of ignorance regarding the consequences of their choices! I will never forget one man who actually told me, "I don't care what treatment or procedure you all give her at this point, as long as whatever it is, she suffers from it."

On the other hand, I have witnessed staggering forgiveness for truly horrendous acts of violence and pain. A man came into the ER one Saturday afternoon with a bullet in his brain, asking to speak with a chaplain. That's right—the man had been shot in the head but was still able to talk and function, at least during the brief time we were able to spend together. Speaking with the man as best I could while the trauma team worked frantically around me, the man told me it was his son who had shot him, but he pleaded with me that I somehow make sure his son knew that he forgave him. The patient must have realized he was not going to make it, and shortly after talking with me he lost consciousness and died. Yet there he was, in what had to have been some of the most difficult and frightening moments of his life, obsessed with extending mercy and forgiveness to the son who had essentially killed him.

I remember a young man who came into the ER, clutching his abdomen so his intestines didn't push out through the stab wound he had sustained at the hands of his brother—a fact that we only found out through other family members because the patient adamantly refused to name his assailant.

I found myself infuriated with the daughter of one of my hospice patients who was so caught up in her own seemingly petty pains and problems that she was unwilling or unable to be there in any manner for her dying mother. Yet her mother, Andrea, was extremely forgiving and stoic about the situation, as well as brutally honest when she revealed to me the hidden dynamics of their relationship:

"My daughter has every right to be unconcerned with my welfare right now, if not to downright hate me. Her father abused her as a child, and I was not able to step in and help the situation in any manner. I was selfish and cowardly; I was afraid of what confronting my husband would do to our marriage. On top of it all, I found myself emotionally distancing myself from my daughter over the years, because I could not cope with her accusatory looks and tones when I failed repeatedly to help her. So, my daughter has suffered horrendously, and much of her own inability to be there for me and for others is the wound she carries from my never having been there for her when she needed me most."

I was amazed at Andrea's self-knowledge and candor. I was also somewhat humbled and chastened when I came to understand the deep pain that her daughter must have been struggling with. I asked Andrea if she had ever said any of this to her daughter or asked for her forgiveness.

"Many, many times," Andrea sighed. "I'm not sure she'll ever be able to forgive me. But I have forgiven her for not being able to forgive me. One of us has to make the first move, and the truth is it should have been me anyway, and many, many years ago. Now, all that matters to me is her healing from all this, whether that healing ever involves her forgiving me or not."

Being Able to Say That Which Really Matters

In his book, *The Four Things That Matter Most: A Book about Living*, Ira Byock, M.D., talks about the critical need to ask for and extend forgiveness, not only at the end of life but frequently throughout the course of living. He cites eleven little words that can transform us, ease our dying, and enrich our living: *Please forgive me. I forgive you. Thank you. I love you.* According to Dr. Byock, only after these words have been exchanged sincerely and in a heartfelt manner can we truly say good-bye to one another at the end of life.

I believe that the order in which Byock instructs us to exchange these "four things that matter" is neither arbitrary nor unimportant. My patients and their families have shown me that you have to ask for forgiveness before the contrition you might well be seeking—and deserve!—is actually extended to you. Of course, many of us are not culpable; rather, we may justifiably feel that the harm was done to us. So why would we have to ask forgiveness in situations such as these? What my patients and their loved ones have taught me is it doesn't seem to matter whether you are actually guilty of wrongdoing. Instead, it is important to simply try to understand why the individual who has wounded you might have felt hurt by or disappointed in you in some manner that led to their hurtful behavior.

Sometimes, as in the case of Andrea, our pleas to be forgiven appear to fall on deaf ears—at least for the time being. Yet, asking forgiveness of others can soften their own resolve to remain hurt and aloof from us. And when two parties exchange heartfelt forgiveness with one another, deep expressions of gratitude and love almost always follow.

You might remember my patient Marjorie, who died in bits and pieces from the complications of her diabetes, and her daughter with whom she had a less than ideal relationship. At one point, out of desperation and in exasperation, Marjorie's daughter told me she actually apologized to her mother for never having been the daughter it appeared her mother had wanted. Marjorie, despite the fact that dementia had long since started to claim her, sat bolt upright and looked her daughter in the eye.

"What are you talking about?" she said. "You've been a fine daughter."

"Mom, that's not the impression you've been giving me all these years."

"Maybe not," Marjorie admitted. Then, after a long pause, "Maybe at times I wasn't the best mother either."

Marjorie never actually asked her daughter to forgive her, but her daughter was more than willing to take this statement as an apology of sorts that helped heal their relationship in Marjorie's final days. If Marjorie's daughter had never made the first move, Marjorie might have never offered her daughter her own apology.

Sometimes the dying aren't the ones needing to give or receive forgiveness so much as they are aware that those they will leave behind are suffering from want of reconciliation. One of my hospice patients, Leeann, was an artist whose home was filled with large, brightly colored canvases of idyllic and glorious landscapes that seemed to mirror, in their expansive sense of serenity, beauty and hope—Leeann's own "inner" landscape. She was at peace with her dying as much as anyone could be, but she was still terribly concerned about her adult son.

"When my son was a boy, we attended a church that preached racial segregation and the oppression of women as God's will. My lovely son saw the hypocrisy of it all long before I did. While I was able to leave that church and find a new spiritual home, my son simply walked out of the church and never looked back. He told me he didn't believe in God, which I guess I can accept at some level, because I know God believes in my son. But what I can't accept is that when I die, my son will have few, if any, spiritual resources to help him cope with my passing."

Leeann had tried to talk to her son about her concerns but was told in no uncertain terms that he had no interest in talking about "that kind of stuff."

Still, she told me that she was praying her son might somehow be able to reconcile past grievances with their religious tradition, allowing him to find the spiritual resources that she felt might be able to help him in the future.

One afternoon, I received a sudden call from Leeann asking me to come see her as soon as possible. I arrived at her home two hours later, only to be greeted at the door by her son. It was our first meeting. He said his mother had just fallen into a sound sleep twenty minutes prior to my arrival and that he was loath to wake her, but he added that he actually wanted to talk with me if I could spare a few minutes. Over a cup of coffee, sitting at his mother's bedside, Leeann's son explained to me how angry he had been when his mother had been diagnosed with Stage 4 pancreatic cancer and she'd decided to opt for hospice care rather than fight to stay alive at all costs, as he had hoped. He told me that up until that very morning he had been unable to reconcile himself with the fact that his mother was dying, and he was unable to talk to her about it. When I asked him what had changed, he told me that the night before he'd had an unusual dream that left him with a strange sense of peace. In it, he and his mother were walking together when they came upon an enormous church. His mother wanted to go into the church while the son wanted nothing to do with it. Still, Leeann had insisted on at least seeing the church, and in the dream her son had relented. At the doorway of the church, a large and very beautiful woman in a flowing gown welcomed Leeann and invited her inside what they could see was a very beautiful church filled with ethereal music. The woman turned to Leeann's son and told him that she was sorry but he couldn't go in yet.

"When I woke up, I felt a deep sense that my mother, even though she is dying, is going to somehow be all right. I also feel that somehow I will be all right, too. I have never believed in God—a little old man with a beard punishing bad people and rewarding the good never made much sense to me. I'm still not sure I'll ever believe in God, but somehow seeing that beautiful woman in my dream, welcoming my mother to that church, gave me a profound sense of peace about my mother dying. I'm still terribly sad about it, but it gave me hope that there's someone somewhere waiting to receive her, and that perhaps

I'll see her there again myself. Anyway, I came over this morning and told my mother all about my dream and how it had left me feeling. And then we both hugged one another and had a good cry together."

Leeann slept peacefully throughout our conversation with a tiny smile on her face. I never did find out why Leeann so urgently wanted to see me, as she died a couple days later. Maybe all she wanted was for me to have that last healing conversation with her son.

Knowing What Matters . . . and What Doesn't

Not only have my patients taught me the importance of reconciliation and forgiveness, but they have also taught me the importance of knowing when to walk away. One of my patients, seeing me get upset because a nurse had been rude to me, said, "Don't waste your lovely self on that nonsense, honey. Life is just too short, and you are just too precious."

Another patient, who had been watching me deal with a difficult patient in the next cubicle of the ER, called me over and whispered in my ear, "Walk away from that man right now, young lady. That man isn't looking for help; he's looking for someone to torture. I'm sure you have better things to do with your time than to put up with that nonsense."

The critically sick and dying have an acute sense of when to seek and offer the sort of healing absolution that will make a true and significant difference in the lives of both the "giver" and the "receiver," and when, on the other hand, they are wasting their precious time and limited resources. They have taught me that not every situation is "fixable," that not every individual is amenable to our desire to make things right or to offer them the best of ourselves. My patients have taught me to shake off petty offenses, and that sometimes the best thing to do is to simply walk away.

Lois, an elderly Jewish woman dying from lung cancer, wanted to help me become a good spiritual caregiver even as she was dying, so she gave me some of the best advice on forgiveness I have ever received:

"There are usually only a few big things in this life for which most of us truly need to go digging around and making amends, and we are usually well aware of what these 'big things' are. These are the things we need to put in order, preferably before we find ourselves dying. Everything else I chalk up to human frailty in myself as well as others. And the only really appropriate response for any sort of human frailty is compassion."

Compassion in Action

When I began training to be a chaplain, people were still dying of AIDS in this country on a regular basis. One of my patients, Rasheed, was a gay African American who had been an intravenous drug user and was dying from just about every AIDS-related symptom and ailment you could imagine. Needless to say, his life had been tough. He told me many stories of his childhood on Chicago's South Side, including how he had been abused at the hands of several of his mother's boyfriends, and how he turned to drugs after his family literally disowned him when he told them he was gay. Rasheed had not been dealt a good hand in life. But Rasheed was one of the kindest and gentlest human beings you could ever hope to meet. Whenever I visited, he would insist on taking my face in his hands and bestowing a kiss on my forehead while imparting a blessing upon me.

"My dear," he used to say to me, "when you walked into my room, the Spirit walked in with you." A black man who may well have had reasons to be bitter at the dominant culture, he was forever telling me how good so many white people actually are, perhaps to put me at ease. Rasheed had a rather eclectic cadre of white people whom he admired, including Ronald Reagan and Meryl Streep. He would often tell me how the man who wrote his favorite song, "Amazing Grace," was white. When I would get up to leave, Rasheed would insist on a good-bye kiss and would always tell me, "Remember, my dear, you are a child of God. Walk in peace and in the Spirit."

I would often leave Rasheed's side, wondering who had just taken care of whom. Rasheed had seen and experienced some of the worst that life has to offer: abuse, addiction, abandonment, and terminal illness. Yet for Rasheed, in the words of my mentor Mrs. Jackson, the worst *was* indeed fertile grounds for mercy. Somehow, instead of becoming bitter and hate-filled, Rasheed became suffused with love and mercy, even for those who historically have been viewed as oppressors of his people. Somehow the worst had not crushed his spirit. Rasheed had come through the worst a transformed human being and was moving toward his death fearlessly and at great peace with himself and his world.

I have found that the world is full of women and men like Mrs. Jackson and Rasheed. These are people—usually spiritual folk, often from disadvantaged backgrounds and circumstances—who have experienced great hardship, but have found within themselves a deep reservoir of mercy. They have a lot to teach us about the beauty of a life lived one day at a time with compassion and purpose, despite all its suffering and hardship. They model for us the deep inner resources that can be mustered.

Fertile Ground for Mercy

All kinds of forgiveness have to be granted in order for us to come out on the other side of grief. We have to forgive loved ones for having died and abandoned us. We have to forgive the Higher Power we believe in for having "allowed" our loved one to die. Even if we don't believe in a Higher Power, when death becomes "personal" we all struggle. We struggle to wrap our minds around the forces in this universe that bring death and destruction to our loved ones in what sometimes can seem like an almost random manner; we struggle to come to some peace with that "process." We have to forgive the medical staff who might have made mistakes or appeared thoughtless or gave poor care. We have to forgive friends and family who did not respond in the manner that we would have expected to first our needs and then to our grief. And sometimes we even have to forgive ourselves for any perceived faults, flaws, or shortcomings we committed throughout the duration of our loved one's illness and death.

The following story might also belong in the next chapter on grief, but it is a story about forgiveness—as are many stories about grief and grieving.

Mrs. Taylor was a single mother whose only child had been born with severe heart defects. After numerous operations and a childhood lived in and out of the hospital, her eighteen-year-old son, Josiah, was being enrolled in our hospice program because his heart was beginning to fail. During their admissions interview, Mrs. Taylor was very curt with me, assuring me that her son did not want to see a chaplain; chaplains only served to remind him that he was dying. Nor would she be needing a chaplain's services since her pastor from a local Baptist church had been accompanying her these many years through every twist and turn of her son's illness. Throughout the interview, Mrs. Taylor struck me as an angry and demanding woman. She appeared very used to dealing with medical personnel and very conversant in medical terminology. She was firm, savvy, and aggressive in her role as advocate for her son. I remained with the nurse for about twenty minutes to finish the intake interview. That was the last I saw of Mrs. Taylor.

Three years later, I was called up to the hospital's Intensive Care Unit to speak with a woman, her teen-aged son, and a friend of the family about the condition of the patient they were visiting—the woman's husband and the young man's father. It had become increasingly obvious over the past few days that the man was most likely dying, which the wife seemed to be accepting but the son was mightily resisting. At the family's request I prayed with them and was about to leave when the third visitor—the friend of the family—stepped out of the hospital room to have a word with me.

"Excuse me, Chaplain. I just wanted to thank you for that lovely prayer you offered. I'm sure it will bring great comfort to this family in the future." A bit flustered by this remark, I tried to brush off the woman's praise, but she was having none of it. She fixed her eyes upon me and then asked slowly and deliberately, "You don't recognize me, do you, Chaplain?" Taken aback, I had to admit that I did not recognize her. She smiled and said, "I'm Mrs. Taylor. Remember, Josiah's mom from such and such hospice?"

How did a woman who had met me for a mere twenty minutes, in the middle of the dreadful time when her son was dying, remember and recognize me after three years? That's what I would have wondered prior to my working with the sick and the dying. What I have discovered is that although I have trouble placing all the names and faces of my dying patients' families, their dealings with their nurses, doctor, chaplain, and any other medical personnel are often etched upon their minds and memories for better or for worse and for the rest of their lives.

For a moment I couldn't speak. I did remember Mrs. Taylor, but certainly this could not have been the same person I met three years before. The Mrs. Taylor I had first encountered had been an angry, assertive woman with little time or patience for me or anyone, save her dying child. In fact, even though I never dealt with Mrs. Taylor and her son again, I knew from my medical colleagues that Mrs. Taylor continued to be a demanding advocate for her son right up until the day he died. I knew that there were many conferences and confrontations regarding her son's care, not all of which were resolved favorably or in a friendly manner. In fact, Mrs. Taylor did not leave our hospice program satisfied with how her son had been treated. She had left us very angry.

The Mrs. Taylor now in front of me was calm, centered, soft-spoken, and filled with the sort of inner peace that immediately makes an impression. We went out for a cup of coffee and talked about the intervening years since we first met. She told me how she had spiraled into a deep depression, wondering what, if anything, she had to live for now that her son was dead. Gradually, however, Mrs. Taylor began to realize that even in her grief, others were seeking her out for her wisdom and advice about dealing with their own sick and dying loved ones. She came to realize that over the years she had actually given significant comfort and advice to many of the other families whose children were also in the hospital with Josiah. She also realized that many of those families would lose their children to the diseases they had been fighting.

"When Josiah was alive I couldn't even go near death, mentally or emotionally, in any manner," Mrs. Taylor admitted. "I had to concentrate on keeping my son alive and thinking about all those other children dying in the hospital around us . . . well, I just couldn't even go there. But after Josiah died and I had all that time to myself, I began remembering each one of those little ones who had passed and the grief their families must have endured. I began to see that I wasn't alone in my grief by any means, and that, in fact, many of those families didn't have their children for nearly as long as I had Josiah. Instead of the bitterness I had felt when Josiah died,

I began to experience a profound gratitude in my heart for all the precious years I had my son."

Mrs. Taylor began to realize that she knew a lot about how hospitals worked and about taking care of people after spending all those years at her son's bedside. She also realized that she had a gift for conveying that knowledge to others, as well as for offering comfort to distressed and burdened family members. Deciding to put her knowledge and natural ability to work for others, she went back to college to study nursing. At the time when I met her, she was a nursing assistant at a local hospice, attending college evenings and weekends to complete her bachelor's of nursing degree.

"You know, as a nurse I can see what it's like to have the shoe on the other foot," Mrs. Taylor said with a laugh. "I used to be very critical of nurses, but now I understand how hard they work and how deeply they care about their patients. I also appreciate how little a nurse or a doctor, for that matter, can do in many situations. But I understand those fierce, angry she-lion mothers who come in and make so many demands for their children . . . because I was one of them! I have a lot of patience and compassion for those women, as well as admiration. And they can see how I feel about them, and because of that we can work well together. How about we go back up to that room and you try to have a word with my friend's son about his father? A word from the chaplain would do him good."

When I told Mrs. Taylor that my own intuition told me that the young man was in no mood for talking to anyone that particular afternoon, she just patted my shoulder and said, "No, probably not. But he will remember that you tried to help, and when he looks back on that in the future, it will bring him some healing."

That's when it hit me, and I remembered the words of my mentor, Mrs. Jackson—"even the worst is fertile ground for mercy." Mrs. Taylor had gone through some of the worst that life can hand a person—the death of her only child after years of pain and illness. And out of the "fertile ground" of that immense suffering, Mrs. Taylor had developed deep compassion, insight, understanding, and mercy for others. She had forgiven what life had done to her and embraced a chance at a new life devoted to helping others. The cycle of forgiveness and mercy continued through her actions and her life's work. As a spiritual caregiver, I saw such small miracles almost daily, knowing in the face of inconceivable suffering that "even the worst is fertile ground for mercy."

Chapter Ten

GRIEF

I ORIGINALLY WAVERED as to whether I should write a chapter on grief. Initially, I didn't think I had anything "new" to share with readers. Working with the sick and dying has reinforced my belief that accompanying a loved one through a debilitating terminal illness or losing a loved one to a sudden death are among the most painful and difficult losses we will endure. Coming to terms with the grieving process for such losses is both agonizing and seemingly interminable. And the manner in which we ultimately make some sort of peace out of our pain and loss and sense out of the rest of our lives, will be unique for everyone.

Moreover, much of this book has already been devoted to stories of grief and how various individuals dealt with it. Remember Olivia's mother, whose pain at the death of her three-month-old daughter only worsened over the months, until she was able to channel some of her grief into the creation of comforting crib quilts for other desperately sick and dying babies? Or how about Mrs. Taylor, whose eighteen-year-old son had been in and out of hospitals all his life until he died, and how she went on to become a nurse and an advocate for others whose loved ones were sick and dying? So what more is there to say, really?

Contemplating this, I began to realize that while stories of loss turned into survival and triumph are all well and good and can give tremendous hope to grieving people, we need to honor the long months and hard emotional work that leads to new life. Knowing that there is a light at the end of a very long and dark tunnel can help people get through the tough days of grief. Still, it is important to discuss and honor the actual grieving process—those days and moments when no hope appears in sight and when pain and depression appear to be one's only companions. For that reason, I have decided to write this chapter.

If you are grieving right now, keep in mind that this is the time to be very, very gentle with yourself. Now is not the time to start a diet or commit to huge projects with inflexible deadlines. Do not make big decisions or a sudden change of long-term plans. If only just this once, make your big goal for each day of grieving to just get through the day—one day at a time. And short of doing harm to yourself or others, give yourself whatever little indulgence or comfort you can whenever possible.

Some days will feel better than others, and some days will feel worse than you ever thought humanly possible. You will wonder when and if this pain is ever going to end. Yet, what I have repeatedly experienced is that the pain does begin to lessen; and whether or not people ever do indeed get on with the business of living, life will never be as it used to be—it will be a new and different life. Gently resist the urge to believe that your only possible path to happiness is to be found in your past life; despite all evidence to the contrary, trust that life can and will be good again.

Grief: Inevitable and Unavoidable

If there is one thing that the dying and their loved ones have taught me about living, it is that not only is grief as inevitable and unavoidable as dying, but like death, its visit will be unpredictable and the way each of us expresses it will be unique. There is no right way to grieve in the immediate event of a loved one's death or in the weeks, months, and years to follow.

One of my earliest cases as a chaplain-in-training involved the death of the wife of Dr. Fischer, one of the hospital's most prominent and esteemed physicians. The elderly couple had been together for more than sixty-one years, and yet the physician's initial response to his spouse's death appeared almost stoic, perhaps tempered by his own years of delivering bad news to hundreds of patients and family members. Following protocol to the letter, this elderly doctor, most likely at great personal expense, pushed aside his immediate grief and strove to put the entire ER at ease, knowing how difficult the situation was for them. I watched Dr. Fischer literally talk stunned and tearful staff members through what they should be doing next. And when he got to me, he smiled and said sardonically, "You must be the new chaplain, right? Huh, so now *I* get the chaplain. Well, it's as it should be. Come, Chaplain, let's proceed with this. I suppose this is your first ER case, now, isn't it? Well, if anything good could come out of this horrendous evening, perhaps it will be that I can walk you through this."

Needless to say, I was astonished to find myself being "walked through" my first ER death by the deceased's spouse! And in my ignorance I could have made the mistake of thinking that the physician's cool and precise attention to me and to the rest of the medical staff was a perverse coldness or a lack of love and concern for his wife.

Had I harbored this misconception, it would have been quickly corrected after Dr. Fischer dismissed me for the evening. I accompanied him to the viewing room to be reunited in private with his deceased wife, and no sooner had I closed the door than I heard his heart-rending wail. As his grief continued to pierce through the silence of the ward, there wasn't a dry eye among the ER staff.

I now understand how, when the unthinkable happens, many people take great comfort in knowing what to do and doing it, almost as if on a kind of human "autopilot." I remember the woman who told me in a panic that she never had been with anyone who had died and therefore didn't know what to do now that her husband's death was imminent. In situations of unthinkable grief, people often need to simply be able to do something and to know what that something is. They also often need to hold on to anything that at that moment makes the world seem less horrific and absurd, be that their professional identity, their individual skills, or their compassion for others.

What Grief and Grieving Look Like

I've spoken before of Maggie Callanan, a former hospice nurse who is a remarkably gifted storyteller as well as an astute observer of the needs of the dying and their families. My strong advice to anyone who has a loved one who is dying, or who works with (or wants to work with) the sick and dying is to read her books. In *Final Journeys: A Practical Guide for Bringing Care and Comfort at the End of Life*, Callanan tells a particularly poignant story about what grief and grieving can look like. Right after her husband had died, a patient's wife called Callanan. It was three a.m., and Callanan drove to the couple's house, as was protocol in the event of a death, only to find the house lit up like a Christmas tree, with the deceased man's wife in the middle of their opened garage, frantically potting geraniums in her bathrobe. "I know this looks totally crazy," the grief-stricken wife told Callanan, "but I just have to do this right now!"

This is what grief looks like. It doesn't have to look "normal"—whatever *that* is!—nor does it have to make any sense. Grief just *is*, and, unless the grieving individual is about to hurt him- or herself or someone else, our job as spiritual caregivers is to let grief be and honor the process for whatever it is.

I remember one woman who, upon hearing her husband pronounced dead, walked up to his bedside and slapped him across the face. "That's for leaving me, you bastard," she spat out.

Once, I had a particularly sad case in which a twenty-nine-year-old man came into the ER suffering a massive heart attack. After he died, his young fiancée, in a state of shock, simply could not wrap her mind around what had happened. She kept trying to call him on her cell phone. Every now and then she would bring his picture up on her phone, kiss it, and, pleading with the staff, would try to grab one of us and say, "See, there he is! He's OK. He's going to be OK."

In another particularly poignant case, a man died in the ER from injuries sustained in a car crash. He was catching a ride back from a ballgame with a "friend of a friend"—and a bad friend of a friend at that—who happened to be drunk. Having survived the grisly crash, this "friend of a friend" wasn't even able to tell us the name of his deceased passenger. (Another life lesson here is you want to be very careful who you get in a car with!) It took us hours to identify the victim and then call his mother, an elderly woman who took a taxi alone to the ER at two a.m., only to find herself being told by our medical team that her son was dead. This woman insisted on sitting with her son's body. For more than two hours she sat, neither saying a word nor moving an inch. Finally, at dawn, she picked up her purse and walked out of the ER, without a glance at or a word to anyone.

Helping People Grieve

Most emergency rooms in most hospitals have a little room off to the side somewhere, devoid of pictures, with a bare minimum of furniture, which goes by some sort of euphemistic and ironic name like "the comfort room." In these little rooms, doctors deliver the very worst news that loved ones could hear. The reason the room is usually devoid of pictures or anything extra is because grief-stricken people regularly erupt into a rampage; it is not uncommon for the medical staff to have to duck out of the way of flying chairs or flying punches. Yet, most medical staff are sympathetic to even the more extreme expressions of grief. Once the individual's initial grief and rage are spent, things usually go on as well as they can, with someone eventually putting the room back in order. There have been many occasions in which that someone was me.

Many of us are brought up with a moral code that teaches us that a stiff upper lip and no tears in public are essential for the well-being of society. Yet I have found that often people who suppress their pain or have trouble expressing uncomfortable or extreme emotions are the ones who have the hardest time dealing with grief in the long run.

My own theory about road rage and the broad disintegration of courtesy in this country is that it has a lot to do with the prevalence of increasing numbers of angry, hurting people who lack support systems for their grief and pain. Grief brings up strong emotional reactions that *need* to be expressed, short of causing harm to yourself and others. And wouldn't it be a kinder, gentler world if we were all more understanding of other people's pain?

Grief is not orderly, logical, or pretty, but neither is much of life. In fact, in the midst of witnessing grief, it is helpful to anticipate the worst rather than demand that people behave at their best. Grief can often and easily be compounded by a person's good—or bad—relational dynamics in the past, and many people in grieving say and do things that are unkind or inappropriate.

I know of a woman who told her family members that she was simply too distraught to attend their mother's funeral, and then backed a moving van into the mother's driveway and cleaned out the house while her siblings were at the funeral. On more than one occasion, I have had to calmly inform a patient's grieving loved one that this particular situation, however grievous, does not warrant their verbal abuse and physical threats, whether the abuse and threats are aimed at me, the staff, the patient, or other loved ones. The wisdom expressed by my beloved patient Lois comes back to me in these situations: the only really appropriate response for any sort of human frailty is compassion.

Grief has a timeline of its own, and it will be different for everyone. Often when someone dies after a lingering and debilitating illness, the first emotional response of loved ones isn't grief but relief. People make the mistake of thinking that grief follows death, but very often the grieving process begins with the first signs of physical diminishment or with the unexpected prognosis received as a surprise blow in the doctor's office. In the event of a lingering illness, the patient's loved ones may fall victim to a kind of anticipatory grief that can be wrenching, particularly when the illness slowly claims their loved one's mind, or their ability to respond or interact.

A patient of mine underwent a severe stroke while dying of cancer. During the months that she lay dying, she was unable to move or respond to her husband in any manner. The only blessing in this situation, if you could call it that, was that the doctors were pretty certain that the stroke had been so massive that the woman was essentially in a coma, devoid of cognizance. On the other hand, her husband suffered horrendously. Every time I visited their home, he wept uncontrollably and insisted that he no longer had anything to live for. It was difficult to get him to do even the small tasks involved in caring for his wife because he was so incapacitated by grief. The hospice had to supply extra care for the couple in their home—much of it simply to monitor the grieving husband—as he also refused to let his wife be transferred to the hospital. What followed was a desperately sad situation in which the staff found themselves unable to give much help or comfort.

Communicating with Loved Ones After They Have Died

I have spoken to many grieving people who have found comfort in what they believe to have been messages or communications from their deceased loved ones. Actually, this phenomenon is fairly well known among medical professionals who, predictably, vary in opinion as to its nature and origin. Bill and Judy Guggenheim have done a study on "after-death communication"— a relatively common experience—interviewing over three thousand people who claim to have had communications from their deceased loved ones, documented in their book, *Hello from Heaven*. I would recommend the book to anyone who thinks they're "going crazy" or that "no one is going to believe me" regarding dreams, visions, or messages they believe they have received from their loved ones after they've passed.

You might remember the story of my girlfriend Gail, whose mother had died, and who believed her mother had been trying to communicate her undying love for her at the dining room table on Thanksgiving. Her mother's favorite song suddenly began playing on the radio. You might also remember the story of Doris who still occasionally heard her deceased husband calling her name.

I have heard many such stories, two more of which stand out in my mind. I had a chaplain friend who believes she received a phone call from one of her deceased patients, thanking her for her care. I also know a woman who prayed furiously for the well-being of a kidnap victim who later was discovered dead. However, prior to authorities finding the body, this woman woke one morning to find the kidnap victim standing over her bed, glowing with peace and joy. She touched the woman on the cheek and thanked her for her prayers before disappearing.

People love to hear these stories, and when I tell them, I always pick up a few more from others who are eager to talk about their experiences to a receptive audience. However, I also usually find people who have not had after-death communication experiences with loved ones, and either wish they had or wonder why they, too, were not given such comforting experiences. Please remember that grief and grieving are unique to every individual and that we all will probably grieve—and receive comfort—in our own individual manner.

Some people are simply and honestly not open to the experience of after-life communication. I laughed when one woman told me that her sister had told her, "I believe in life after death, but please do *not* come around trying to talk to me or make the furniture move or anything like that after you pass, because it will just freak me out! When you're dead, just stay away from me, please."

You might be saying, "But I *am* open to communication from my deceased loved ones! Why haven't I had this experience?" If so, I invite you to look back on your time of grief and look at instances that might have been more subtle forms of communication from a deceased loved one. I recall one woman who had a lovable and eccentric aunt who loved to drink White Russians. When her aunt died, the woman was stationed overseas with her husband and unable to get back to the funeral. So, it occurred to her to pour herself a White Russian and drink a toast to her aunt.

I think we often get the idea to do something at the gentle prodding of those spirits and deceased loved ones who still care so very much about our continuing earthly journey, even though they are no longer with us in the flesh. Many times I believe my deceased patients have given me a gentle nudge to do a certain thing or to listen to an "intuition" regarding a suffering patient or family member. We can honor these communications for what they might well be—loving assistance from another plane of existence. Increasingly, we are becoming aware of the interconnectedness of all being. Therefore, we can be thankful that we are, in fact, *not* alone in anything, be it our crowning achievements or our worst moments.

Perhaps the most difficult time for grieving individuals is those lonely days when there is no obvious "after-death communication" going on; rather, we acutely feel the absence, but not the presence, of a loved one. Again, this is the time to be very, very gentle with ourselves. Allow time to be alone and cry. Forgive ourselves for not "getting on with life" as quickly as other people might suggest would help *them* deal with *their* grief. On the other hand, we can be on the lookout for, and not turn down, opportunities that might distract us from or even lessen our grief for a while. We can think of what has made us happy, peaceful, and energized before this horrendous grief, and endeavor to accept similar opportunities once more.

The Possibility of a Life Beyond Grief

I provided grief counseling for Mina, a woman whose son was killed in a car accident. Mina went to the cemetery every day to visit her son's grave. This is not unusual, but what was perhaps unique about her grief was that she had a profound need to feed her dead son. Feeding him had been one of her key joys in life as a mother, as her son proved to be a voracious and appreciative eater. So Mina brought bowls of her son's favorite soup to the graveyard and, while sobbing, would ladle spoonfuls onto his grave.

Eventually the attendants at the cemetery discovered and forbade Mina to continue bringing food to her son's grave, threatening to ban her from entering the cemetery if she didn't comply. Their concern was that the food on the grave attracted rodents and other pests, but nothing and nobody seemed able to convince this grieving mother to stop pouring food on her son's grave.

After talking with the officials at the cemetery, pleading for a bit of leniency and assuring them that I was working with this grieving mother, we were able to come up with some other outlets for Mina's broken heart and emotional turmoil. I suggested she place a bowl of soup in front of her son's portrait in their living room from time to time, allowing him to "enjoy" her home cooking in the privacy of their home. Some of her son's friends providentially decided to sponsor a fundraiser to set up a memorial scholarship at her son's high school, and so as a "mother" again she was able to throw herself into cooking for the event. Mina was a fine cook, and all the food she brought quickly sold out. From there she received several inquiries about putting her cooking skills to good use—one from the manager of a soup kitchen and another from a volunteer coordinator at the local Ronald McDonald House. Soon, this grieving mother was not only cooking for the families of desperately ill children and homeless families, but with the passing months, she developed a social network that helped give new meaning to her life.

Yet despite her having found new outlets for her grief, I was surprised to learn that Mina had, in fact, never stopped bringing food to her son's grave. "Now I only bring a spoonful or two in a tiny jar and pour it over his grave when I leave and no one's looking," she told me with an almost mischievous smile. When a grieving mother smiles like that, you know that deep healing is happening.

One of my former college professors, Robert Schreiter, is a world-renowned expert on reconciliation and healing. He has traveled all over the globe, helping to facilitate reconciliation in places as far away as South Africa, Rwanda, and Balkan countries. Often he would talk about how many victims of war, having experienced horrendous atrocities and torture, now had a "survivor mission." They were committed to help bring healing to themselves or others, to help victims forgive those who had harmed them, and therefore move beyond their grief.

I have always thought that the individuals who do best after the death of a loved one, who come through the process of their own grief, stronger and at peace, are those with their own kind of "survivor mission." Olivia's mother comes to mind, with her ministry of making baby quilts for other grieving mothers, as does Itedal, who made it her mission that the hospital where her husband died had an imam on hand for other Muslim patients.

Another person with a particularly powerful and poignant survivor mission was Paula, a woman of European-American heritage who had married a Latino gentleman with whom she had twin girls. The couple divorced and the twin girls grew up with Paula. The girls had very distinct Latino features and consequently experienced racism that shocked and appalled their mother. In fact, had she not been privy to it through her own flesh and blood, she might not have believed it. Nonetheless, the girls had friends of all races and ethnicities, and when they died tragically in a car crash, Paula held a memorial service that not only welcomed the girls' great diversity of friends, but gave them a place to grieve through music and poetry from their own backgrounds and of their own making. In honor of her daughters and their experience, Paula went on to support, encourage, and mentor many other young people of a variety of backgrounds long after her daughters had died.

The Importance of Self-Care

Last but not least, if we are taking care of someone who is grieving, we must take very, very good care of ourselves. Grief—even someone else's—can literally suck the life out of us and make us vulnerable to a kind of spiraling negativity that can prove difficult to let go of. Likewise, anyone who works with the critically ill and dying over the long haul is subject to accumulated, unresolved grief manifesting as anger, depression, sarcasm, various forms of substance abuse, an overall judgmental attitude towards others, and, ultimately, burnout. Issues of unresolved grief may explain why so many doctors and nurses can seem so angry, blunt, and uncaring.

Gloria, a family friend who was studying to be a chaplain, wound up in the hospital with a broken leg and a concussion due to a bad fall. While in the hospital, she received a visit from the chaplain. She told him that she, too, wanted to be a chaplain because she loved helping people. The chaplain replied sarcastically, "If you want to feel good about helping people, go work at Wal-Mart." Naturally, my friend was angry and hurt to be spoken to in such a manner, but I'm guessing the poor chaplain just needed a sabbatical. The problem is that medical personnel don't get sabbaticals. In fact, the people who do some of the most important work there is to do—caring for our sick and dying loved ones—are very often overworked and unable to get the rest and rejuvenation that would make a major difference in the quality of compassionate care they could continue giving. Ours is a medical system in woeful need of an overhaul.

Practicing self-care and being very kind and gentle with ourselves in times of grief will help us find and receive the kind of inner healing that helps us go on. Self-care will deepen our own capacity to care for others. This inner healing comes through many different ways and means: It can come through rest, prayer, getting out in nature, listening to music, making things, meditating, or being with a special animal or human friend. We must not neglect these recreative pursuits which literally can assist in "re-creating" a broken heart and an injured spirit. We must be intentional about listening to and attending our grief. We are worth it.

Chapter Eleven

LOVE

I WAS OUT TO DINNER WITH A DEAR FRIEND and her husband. We were at a new restaurant I had been eager to try for weeks, however, instead of enjoying myself, I munched away at my dinner, furious.

My husband, Stephen, who was supposed to have met the three of us for dinner after work, showed up an hour and a half late. I couldn't wait for him to join us so I could kill him. My friends, knowing I was none too happy, tried to lighten my mood. However, nothing they could have said would have softened my rage. I knew why Stephen was late: he obviously had been with a patient who had taken more time than he'd expected, and he'd neglected to call me about it. This is how my husband operated and, ironically, it was one of the reasons I fell so in love with him.

When Stephen was with a patient and family, they had his undivided attention. Phones could ring, pagers could go off, but he virtually ignored them, providing loving and tender care for the person at hand as if the man or woman were the only one on the planet.

Who wouldn't fall in love with a man like that . . . until he winds up being your husband and you're the one on the other end of that unanswered phone call or pager! Yet by Stephen's thinking, the person in front of him commanded his complete and utter attention. The American habit of interrupting conversations to retrieve pages and answer phone calls both baffled and annoyed my Irish-born husband.

We were contemplating desserts and coffee when, at last, Stephen flopped himself down at the table, looking both sheepish and spent. I gave him my best cold shoulder, while my girlfriend and her husband inquired about his day.

"Actually," he told them, glancing at me warily, "this man came in to talk to a chaplain right as I was locking up the office for the day. He wasn't a patient or a family member, but he was so distraught that I realized I just couldn't brush him off and send him down to the ER to talk with a social worker. So, I sat him down in the office. After telling me a long, sad story about his addictions, his failed relationships, and his emotional pain, he pulled out a rather large knife and said to me, 'You know, sometimes, I just feel like hurting someone.'"

My friends and I were speechless.

"So what on earth did you do?" I finally asked.

Stephen shrugged. "I just said to him, 'Oh no, you don't want to hurt anybody with that knife. That's why you came to see a chaplain now, isn't it? You're here now so I wouldn't let you hurt yourself or anyone else, isn't that right?' And then the man just burst out sobbing, so we had ourselves a little talk together."

During this "little talk," Stephen was able to convince the man to surrender his weapon, but he also eventually talked the man into voluntarily admitting himself to the hospital's psychiatric unit, walking him up to the admittance desk himself! And after Stephen had told us this story, all the while having furtively perused the menu, he announced "I know you're probably ready to leave, but I'm rather hungry after all that. Would anyone mind if I just got a sandwich?"

Now, when my husband is late getting home from work or when he neglects to answer my pages in as timely a manner as I might hope, I let go of my anger and irritation. I am the one at fault if I let these small annoyances rob me of the other pleasures of the day—like a good meal at a fine restaurant or the company of old friends. Looking back on that frightening day when my husband was approached by an unstable man with a large knife, I see that the evening gave me one of the most precious memories and insights I'll ever have—that my husband is a very brave and loving man who was willing to put his own life on the line to help someone in need. That evening also reminded me that one of these evenings my husband may not come home at all, because he might in fact be unable to do so. The reality is that we do not know when or how our loved ones will meet death, and every moment we have with them is to be treasured. The fact that our loved ones will die makes it all the more poignant and compelling to love them every moment of every day as though it were their last.

I wish I could tell you that it was my experience with the dying that made me see how truly precious every moment is with our loved ones. But it was facing the possibility of my own loved one's sudden and violent death that drove home to me the need to cherish every minute we are privileged to experience the deep joy and wonder of love, and being loved. And yet the dying have given me a very special gift too—a deeper understanding of what love truly is, and what loving really looks like.

What Does Love Really Look Like?

In working with the dying, we get so familiar with death that we can almost feel and recognize its presence when it slips into a hospital room or takes its place beside a hospice bed. What does constant exposure to death and dying do to people who are the caregivers of the sick and dying? Caring for the dying has the ability to shut us down emotionally or open us up to new levels of living and loving. In my husband's case, I believe that working with the dying has given him a nearly fearless disregard for his own well-being in favor of the pressing and immediate needs of the individual in front of him. This is, by no means, an abandonment of all common sense in the face of threat or danger. It is seeing and responding to the human need and suffering at hand rather than allowing fear, and the danger of any given situation, to dictate his ultimate response. The dying have taught me that this is what love looks like—a literal laying down of our life for another.

Seeing and working with so much death and dying lessens our fear of death and strengthens our intuitive understanding. In the case of the man with the knife, my husband told me that he didn't experience much outright fear or concern. Stephen simply sensed that if he remained calm and addressed the issues at hand, the situation would turn out OK. He also didn't feel the police needed to be summoned or involved, since he felt the real problem wasn't that this individual had a criminal intent to harm others. Instead, he could see this man was in deep emotional pain. Locking him up in the criminal justice system meant he would not get those psychological issues at the heart of his inner pain addressed—locking him down temporarily in a psych unit meant he could get counseling, medication, and care. When this man was released, there would be a follow-up plan, and doctors and social workers to meet with him, should he choose to do so. Rather than demonizing the man, Stephen and the other caregivers at the hospital were able to respond to him as an individual in dire need of help and immediate care. It is this kind of unselfish love that allows first responders and emergency medical personnel to enter tense and dangerous situations every day, for the purpose of caring for others and saving lives.

The Fleeting Nature of Material Possessions

Death does not respect any age. Neither does it value or spare individuals based on the number of people who love them or according to some perceived value system of the person's "usefulness" to society. I have seen people of all ages die, some who have lived only hours or a few years. I have no answers as to why death takes some people earlier than others, or why some people linger way beyond what makes sense to them, due to their advanced years and diminished abilities. I have accompanied too many women who have lost their husbands way too young—like the young father who died riding the motorcycle he had gotten for his birthday, a mere twenty minutes after he had first mounted it, or the man who was feeling ill on his honeymoon and came back to be diagnosed with an inoperable brain tumor. I have watched too many parents lose a child, and too many children lose their parents way before their parenting duties were fulfilled.

What all this death and dying reminds me is that today is the day to love your loved one fiercely and uncompromisingly, as though today might be their last day on Earth. And if either of you has a dream or something that you would like to do together that would give you a priceless and enduring memory, do not put that dream off for some distant day in the future. It might never come. If it is at all possible to do so, do it now.

The dying have shown me that we do not need expensive furniture, nice "toys," or a big house. These things cannot love us back, and we certainly can't take them with us. Without compromising what future we might have, and without failing to make some financial provisions for that future, I have learned that *now* is the only time to take those "dream trips" with our loved ones, and that those "dream trips" don't have to be extravagant adventures costing a fortune. A "dream trip" can be as simple as an impromptu picnic during the week after work, packing up to head to the beach on a Tuesday evening to walk through the waves at sunset, or surprising our loved ones with a weekend away at a bed and breakfast that will pamper us both a bit. It can be a night out at a jazz club or surprising our loved ones with a hot air balloon ride or an afternoon learning to ride a horse. Dream trips and priceless memories happen when we listen to the longings of our loved ones' hearts and respond generously to those longings. In other words, we can and should have "dream trips" with our loved ones as often as possible.

I have had the opportunity to listen to many dying people share their "dream trips." I have also listened to the loved ones of many a departed patient express to me how grateful they were for a certain precious memory, or memories—which often they helped create. Sometimes those memories *are* of big trips—safaris, ocean cruises, or trips to some foreign country that were anticipated and planned for years. Yet just as often, those memories are of a surprise bouquet of roses that arrived for no special occasion, a kiss or cuddle on the couch in front of the TV that resulted in shutting the program off, a special family gathering filled with laughter and affection, or even just a walk together that resulted in a chance encounter at twilight with a small herd of deer or an owl perched on a nearby tree limb. People often tell me of the liminal quality of their memories of these sorts of events, giving deep comfort and healing to their hearts, almost as if their loved ones were still alive within those memories, loving them back.

Having lots of money and many possessions often has very little to do with how we die. I have had the privilege to work at one of the finest hospitals in America, which catered to many of Chicago's rich and elite. I have also been privileged to work for hospitals largely serving the urban poor. I have had my car parked by valets and doors held opened by doormen, as I've made my way to luxury condos filled with priceless art and expensive furnishings and stunning wrap-around views of Lake Michigan out the living room windows. I have also traveled to impoverished neighborhoods filled with the abandoned carcasses of old homes, to sit at the bedside of people literally dying in squalor. Yet, there is very little difference, based on their finances, in how one dies. Money may buy more of some types of medical care, but it cannot buy peace of mind, relief from emotional turmoil or spiritual angst, loved ones to hold one's hands, or even another moment of life. I have watched wealthy people die with no one but the maid and the hired nurse looking in on them from time to time, and I have watched near penniless women and men die surrounded by large and loving extended families. Those who meet death with dignity, hope, and comfort, surrounded by people who care deeply for them, are usually those who have loved well and have been loved back.

Nothing Is More Important than Loving and Being Loved

The dying have taught me that nothing is more important in this life than love. In fact, we will look back and stand in judgment of our own lives based largely on how we have loved and were loved. When I use the term "stand in judgment," I am not referring to some other being—earthly, divine, or otherwise—ultimately judging our lives and rewarding or condemning us "appropriately." First of all, my own beliefs—and these are *my* beliefs based upon my own work with the dying—are that there is a Divine Being and that this Divine Being is all Love. Why would I think that this Divine Being is "all love" and not some celestial tally keeper waiting to hand out justice and rewards? It is because I have watched so many people ultimately die well, meaning healed of their large and small hatreds, their fears, their pettiness, and their anxiety, not because of how they have lived but almost in spite of how they have lived.

In terms of our ability to meet death with less regret and more inner peace, those of us who have loved generously and lavishly for much of our lives might have an advantage over those of us who have withheld love, or done actual physical and emotional harm to others. Also, those who have loved generously and lavishly quite often find themselves cared for in their final months and hours by those very people to whom they devoted such love and care. Yet, anyone—at any point in their lives—can change their heart and strive to live a life of love in earnest. The Divine Being running the universe appears to honor this change of heart—or even simply our desire for a change of heart—and grants lavish clemency and assistance to anyone seeking to live a more generous life.

Ultimately, it is we who judge ourselves and, more often than not, I believe, we judge far more harshly than is "appropriate." As we discovered together earlier in this chapter, people wielding big knives are often in considerable emotional pain, even mentally ill, or psychologically impaired. Life is very difficult, and most of us will reach the end of it bruised and battered, with any number of emotional wounds and significant disappointments, having loved and lived deeply far less than we potentially could have. Yet knowing that nothing is, ultimately, more important than loving and being loved, could we not now begin to make changes that might assist us, on our death beds, in looking back on our lives with minimal regret?

Love is worth the risk. It is worth going after, time and time again. I have had the opportunity to hear many stories of love found late in life, or by happy accident, or, more poignantly, after the death of a beloved spouse or child. I know of a loving couple that only met because their deceased spouses were buried next to one another. I know of several couples who got married after meeting at bereavement groups for parents who had lost a child. I know of people who have found love and married for the first time at the ages of 52, 65, 71, 84, 87, and 93!

I have known people who have had the children they had longed for—though they'd been unable to conceive—through marriage to a spouse who brought children to their union. Time after time I have seen people who thought their lives were over after losing their beloved partner or child, only to find love in the most unexpected of places and with the most unlikely of people. It doesn't matter if you have years or months or merely days left to live. There isn't a single one of us who can know for certain when their last moment on this Earth will be, so while we still have the time and the opportunity, why not choose love?

Choose Love—and Walk Away from Everything Else!

What has greatly impressed me about the dying is their ease in detaching from anything that is a waste of their precious remaining hours. Having reached an uneasy acceptance of their impending death, many people have little patience for dishonesty or duplicity. Perhaps because facing our mortality head-on has a way of exposing the façade of shallowness and the veneer of "niceness" under which so many of us live our lives, dying people often intuit who's "being real" with them and who's not. They often opt to spend their remaining time dealing with those individuals who are "being real," while appearing overly blunt and impolite with others who want to maintain the illusion of a life moving along smoothly.

At the end of life, many people have confessed to me that nothing is more alienating and enraging than having the people around them insist that "everything's going to be all right" when, in fact, they know in their heart of hearts that they are dying, and that nothing is ever going to be the same again. Granted, it can be very difficult to care for someone, or sit with someone and admit that things are going from bad to worse. It can be like looking in a mirror and getting a glimpse of our own mortality—something many of us do everything possible to avoid. Yet, it is exactly this type of brave and unselfish loving that the dying need from us.

In this life we will encounter a great many people telling us that they like or even love us when, in reality, they couldn't care less. In fact, what they might "love" about us is how good we make them feel, either because they can hurt us or feel superior, or manipulate us to behave or react in a manner that pleases, suits, or justifies them and their actions. We know who these people are and what they look like: the ever smiling coworker who has acquired our "allegiance" like an insurance policy against her own insecurity or to bolster up his own worldview. Or it might be that "friend" for whom we merely serve as an audience, witnessing his dramas or her successes. Or it's that "kindly" relative who always has the poison remark ready when no one else is within earshot. These people always have an underlying edge to their comments or an ever so slightly biting observation to make. These people would swear on their own deathbeds that they feel nothing but love and goodwill toward us, and were we to doubt it, well, how mean, unfair, and misguided *we* would be!

In truth, these people are classic manipulators who spend a great deal of their time trying to get themselves and others to see how great they are *and* how bad, unfair, unkind—fill in the blanks with any other aspersions—we are. The dying have taught me to walk away from these people, and to *not look back*. Is this an "unloving" response? Not at all! Letting people know that we will neither tolerate being treated poorly nor let them waste our time on habitually toxic encounters is one of the most loving things we can do for them. It can invite them to think about why we are no longer interested in being in their life, and perhaps even change their behavior in a manner that will truly benefit them in the long run. No one benefits from living a lie, not even the person for whom it *seems* to have had a short-term benefit.

If these are people who cannot be walked away from easily—because, say, we're related to them by blood or marriage—limit the time with them. And know this: there are a great many people in this world who do know how to love, and who have love that they would be happy to share with us. We can find *these* people and make *them* our friends and family.

What Loving Looks Like When Things Get Difficult

I have dealt with hundreds of families and have seen all kinds of family dynamics played out around sickbeds and deathbeds. A classic scenario involves the scapegoating of one family member by other family members. Love has fallen short in some manner; it has not been extended sufficiently, or has been withdrawn, or was only given conditionally. I will hear all about and be warned of this "black sheep," and on occasion this individual will indeed turn out to be a truly troublesome individual with little ability to give and receive anything beyond his or her own small universe of self-concern. Yet, even though some people can ultimately turn out to be truly thoughtless and selfish adults, we need to remember that if we tell anyone long enough that they are bad, chances are they will be. The truth of the matter is that people become what we tell them we think they are, either implicitly or explicitly. But the interesting thing is that this is usually not the case at all with the family members who are the "black sheep."

Often the member of the family who gets scapegoated is the one who, like many of the dying, sees the forest from the trees and no longer wants to play a game of hide and seek in the woods. In other words, they are refusing to live the lies and the deception that other family members have created and are trying desperately to maintain. Usually such scapegoats are the first to see that the family matriarch is dying rather than "looking better every day," or they are the ones insisting that "Dad didn't want a breathing tube put down his throat" when everybody else is looking to extend Dad's life in any way possible despite "Dad's" wishes to the contrary. More often than not, the "black sheep" are the family members who understand love and take love to a different level, knowing that to love honestly, selflessly, and without reservations is often a very difficult business.

If we really don't love someone, or if we love someone but don't feel up to the task of accompanying that person through their illness in an honest and truly caring manner largely devoid of the temptation to try to meet our own needs first, then the best thing we can do is to get out of the way. We need to leave the bulk of the care for this person to someone else. That is the truly most loving thing we can do.

I once encountered a woman who was livid with me for witnessing her ex-husband's health-care policy that gave complete power of attorney to his girlfriend. The woman's fury went so far as to pressure the administration to revoke the power of attorney form, but, of course, there was no doing that because her ex-husband had made his decision while of sound mind and body. In fact, he was so desperate to get it down on paper that his ex-wife would *not* in any way have power of attorney over him that I suspect *he* suspected he would be deprived of the best care or consideration from his ex-wife were she to have any power over him or his medical care. The ex-wife ranted and raved that her ex-husband's girlfriend had stolen her husband from her, that the girlfriend was very manipulative in nagging the man into making her his power of attorney—all of which insinuations may have been 100 percent accurate. Also, for all I know, this woman's ex-husband could have been a philandering creep. However, that does not negate the fact that the man had a right to assign his power of attorney to anyone he wanted. I advised the ex-wife that perhaps it was time for her to let go of her ex-husband and move on, which was not what she wanted to hear. But this is indeed what each and every one of us needs to hear: When our anger at a person—or our affronted sense of justice—outweighs our compassion and concern for them and their well-being, someone else needs to step in to be their primary caregiver. This is what real love looks like.

Perhaps we are not greatly concerned about love; we may wish the dying person to suffer. Maybe this person beat you within an inch of your life when you were a child, or was roaring drunk at every holiday gathering, or stole your spouse and absconded with your hard-earned fortune. Many family members have intimated to me that they were upset their dying loved ones didn't seem sorry enough or weren't suffering enough. I would remind them that, not to worry, their loved ones were indeed "suffering enough." After all, they were dying.

Love's Eternal Nature

The love we experience on this plane does not end; it goes on after death. In fact, in some cases, it gets better with the death of our loved one, but not merely because the departed person has stopped hurting or disappointing us. As I have pointed out earlier, many people believe they have received signs and messages from their loved ones after they have died. Many continue to love their loved ones long after they have passed, and many feel "loved back." I believe our departed loved ones continue to look out for us and guide us throughout our lifetime, and that we can benefit from their guidance, even grow in our love for and understanding of our departed loves, though they are not physically present. I believe this because I have watched how many people have been able to forgive their departed loved ones for past hurts, despite the fact that those loved ones are dead. As we grow older, we not only come to understand more and more how difficult life can be, but we can appreciate, through our own faults and foibles, how easy it is to hurt others inadvertently out of our own suffering. It is a gift to know that we can forgive and ask forgiveness of those who have preceded us in death, and, if we listen silently and patiently with our hearts, we can eventually feel their gratitude and forgiveness extended back to us. We can experience powerful emotional freedom by wishing the very best for our loved ones, especially the ones who wounded us deeply.

Love: The Only Thing Worth Building Our Lives Upon

Love is truly the only thing worth building our lives upon. Whether it is the loving relationship of a committed partnership, or the love that is nurtured between an adult and a child, or love between friends, or the love that manifests in service to others, love is really all that matters. In fact, a life built upon love will slowly but surely blossom into a deeper, purer way of living, yielding yet more love, more compassionate thoughts and actions with each passing year.

In writings of the Torah, the Jewish people came to experience a special kind of love known as *hesed*, which roughly translates to a merciful loving-kindness that manifests itself in works of mercy and justice, especially for the poor and the downtrodden of this world. When we work in end-of-life care, we open ourselves to an environment ripe for the growth and blossoming of this kind of deep, pure love—within ourselves, as well as in the hearts and lives of those around us. It is love that's pure joy, manifesting everywhere, not merely in our immediate friends or family. It is the type of love that survives even the deaths of those we love most. It is the type of love that can give new meaning to lives that have been destroyed by death's ravages and new energy to broken hearts. The Jewish people, however, did not believe that *hesed* had its origins in the human heart. They believed that this love was and remains a love between Divine Love and human love. Looking back, I have come to know and admire many fine people—doctors, nurses, and other caregivers—who have devoted their lives to serving others, and who appear to emanate this sort of selfless and deeply merciful loving-kindness. I believe it is this sort of love that so many caregivers manifest—a love that is both beyond us and yet deeply within us, the source and well-spring of the unending love each of us has the opportunity to experience, and ultimately the only thing worth building our lives upon.

Chapter Twelve

WHAT ARE YOU DOING
WITH THE REST OF YOUR LIFE?

WORKING WITH THE DYING deeply changes our questions and perspective. For instance, one out of every six people on this planet—roughly one billion people—live in extreme poverty? Day in and day out, their chief preoccupation is simply finding enough food to stay alive. For another billion men and women, gaining access to rudimentary health care, clean drinking water, basic education, and safe shelter constitute their major daily preoccupations. Therefore, roughly one in three people on this planet struggle mightily just to make it through life. Why is it that you or I were not born one of these people in such abject and challenging living conditions?

Similarly, working in health care shifts our assumptions and perceptions about life. When people of all ages—all around us—are dying, we begin asking some important questions: 'Why am I still alive? Why haven't I gotten cancer yet or been hit by a drunk driver while heading home after work? Why was I born relatively healthy? Why do I wake up most mornings pain-free? Why was I born able to breathe without the assistance of a machine? Why is it that I am still able to walk across a room unassisted, or feed myself, rather than struggle to control my muscles and my movement?'

We no longer assume that living into our mid-eighties is our birthright or that we're likely to move through life with nothing more serious than a tummy tuck or a knee replacement as our "chief medical concern." We also begin to understand that good health is not necessarily a given. Rather than smoking three packages of cigarettes a day or carrying around an extra hundred pounds, we learn there are things we can do to maximize our odds of living a longer, healthier life. Still, it's really about maximizing "odds," not certainties.

I have learned humility while staring into the face of powers that are lethal and well beyond anyone's ability to control. More and more I have to realize that every day of being alive and healthy is a tremendous gift not to be taken lightly. And the gift of being alive and healthy is the type of gift best enjoyed when shared.

Working with other health-care professionals, it becomes clear that most of them do not leave their very demanding day jobs and simply stop thinking about the medical needs of others at the end of their shifts. Many dedicated caregivers spend nights and weekends working at free clinics or collecting medical supplies to send to poor hospitals at home and abroad. They likewise spend their vacations in distant countries performing free, life-giving surgeries for desperately poor people who would have otherwise suffered without care. Often they work, for no salary, shoulder to shoulder with other health-care professionals in Third World countries, sharing with them and teaching them new surgical techniques learned in First World countries.

I have come to believe that once we are able to see the power of positive action in the face of suffering, illness, and disease, we become more and more eager and willing to spend ourselves—our good health and good fortune, our medical skills and our free time—on making the world a better place. This is why so many people who give of themselves just keep on giving more and more. And this kind of positive response to the world's ills makes our own lives infinitely sweeter, richer, and more rewarding. We become happier, with a positive outlook on life, taking very little for granted, experiencing over time deepening levels of gratitude and enjoyment in even the most minor of life's delights. We are doing some good for the planet, true enough, but the good we are doing is doing *us* good.

The Good We Do and the Love We Give Is of Inestimable Value

I have learned that the good we put into this world is never forgotten, even if we forget it. Good multiplies and brings about more good. Take the task of sitting with a dying person and holding his hand. The janitor comes in to clean the room, and, upon seeing you there, she realizes you must be accompanying someone who is actively dying. The janitor takes the time to say a prayer of her own for the patient. (Do not doubt for a minute that some of the most effective "chaplains" and "caregivers" in the hospital are the housekeeping staff. Take the time to acknowledge and befriend them when you or your loved one enter a hospital and you will not regret it.)

The nurse comes in and she sees you sitting there and is reminded, despite her hectic schedule and relentless pace, to slow down just a little bit. Perhaps she forgot for a moment why it is that she became a nurse—not only to monitor machines and fill out charts, but to give very tender and direct care to the sick and dying. Because she was able to slow down, she goes into the next room and gives better care to another patient. That patient, receiving her good care, feels better both physically and emotionally, and when the patient's spouse and children come in that evening to visit, she is able to have a loving and productive conversation about their plan of care and impending discharge. One of the patient's children, seeing how lovingly his parent is being cared for, begins to contemplate a career in health care.

But, for a minute, let's go back to the room and the bedside chair where you are sitting with a dying patient. After you have sat with, prayed for, and physically comforted that dying patient—swabbing his dry mouth with water, adjusting his pillow ever so slightly so he can breathe better—that patient dies. But let me tell you something that I know by experience, if not by proven fact: That patient does not simply die and forget you. That patient moves on to another plane of existence where, in gratitude and in a spirit of profound love, that individual is able to now offer you assistance on your life's journey. Sounds like a fairy tale, doesn't it? But I believe there is nothing truer in this life—that we can and do receive love and assistance from those who have "passed on."

You might say to yourself: "This sounds plausible in terms of our loved ones carrying on a relationship with us after death, but how is it that people who received, let's say, three hours worth of care at best would even bother to help an otherwise virtual stranger after passing on, even if they were at all able to? Haven't they got a whole slew of loved ones they knew and loved all their life whom they would rather spend their loving attention on?"

Let me answer that question with another question: If you had been in a serious accident and had learned that, while unconscious, a stranger had pulled you from the burning wreckage of your car and summoned an ambulance before continuing on with her own journey, how would *you* feel about *that* stranger? From the dying I have learned that this thing we call love—in this life and on this plane of existence—is a very small thing compared to the size and the scope of the love our departed patients and loved ones have at their disposal.

At this point in the book, you may think that I am advocating that everyone become a medical professional in order to make this a better world, but let me say that nothing could be further from the truth. What I am advocating, instead, is that we all consider spending whatever time is ours to spend putting good into this world in whatever manner best fits our gifts, temperament, and abilities. And we can often identify our unique gifts and abilities by following our heart—to sense what is either missing from our life or what we are truly passionate about.

Every one of us is unique in the contributions that we can make. What's more, we can come to recognize that "uniqueness" and the subsequent "response" we can make with our life choices. This recognition is often best found in dialogue with death, life's greatest teacher, and with the dying. The urgencies of our heart are more clearly heard when death is imminent and when being with the dying forces us to face our own mortality.

I would like to go back to a story from the first chapter, the story of Helen, a seventy-something patient who was dying of cancer. Helen had been single and worked as an executive secretary until she married a widower when she was in her mid-fifties. At that point, she started traveling the globe with her new husband. Helen kept a large map in her living room with pushpins at all the exotic locations she and her husband had visited. She spent a lot of her time with me, showing me all the pictures and souvenirs of her overseas trips. Helen also embarked upon a very successful second career in painting; her home was full of beautiful landscapes and still-lifes of gorgeous, colorful flowers. Even though she was dying, she radiated a deep satisfaction with the life she'd enjoyed, and she was largely at peace with her impending death.

As I explained in the first chapter, I always left Helen's house a bit unsettled, and I eventually came to terms with the fact that I was jealous—which turned out to be a precious gift, because my jealousy signaled what was missing from my life, and what it was that I was truly passionate about.

In sharing my time with this dying woman, I realized that I was really missing having a partner in life. Desiring a life partner is not a selfish impulse: my husband and I have both come to realize that, as a happily married couple, we are able to give much more of ourselves than we ever were able to while we were single. My interactions with this elderly woman also made me realize that I had neglected developing my artistic talents in favor of building my career. If I were to receive a terminal prognosis tomorrow, one of the things I would regret was not having traveled more.

Each of Us Has a Unique Story

After examining what was missing from my life by comparing it to my dying patient Helen's life, I hastened to bring more balance into my daily living and set aside the time and space to meet people who might potentially be good-life partners. The irony is, of course, that while I went out and met many men through a whole variety of singles-oriented events that any large city offers, the man I ultimately married I met while working with the sick and dying.

Stephen and I grew to admire one another by engaging in the sort of work that tested us emotionally, physically, and spiritually on a daily basis. Interacting with my future husband in tense situations that demanded selflessness showed me his true character, so there were very few surprises once we were married. I may not recommend a career in medicine for all my readers, but I would definitely recommend looking for a life partner through volunteer work, or by involving yourself in any sort of work for the sick, the poor, the homeless, the disadvantaged, and the dying. The people you will meet involved in these initiatives are the sort of people who usually make generous and caring life partners. And the partner I ultimately found through my work with the dying not only proved to be a wonderful man, but was, just as importantly, a man who understood me and my work, and who valued me tremendously.

The next objective I sought in improving balance and meaning in my life was to take art lessons. I did this not so much because I wanted or needed art lessons per se, but rather to be more accountable for showing up somewhere and actually doing something creative on a regular basis. My artistic abilities were rusty to say the least, but after taking several classes, not only was my confidence in my ability to create restored, but the energy it takes to create art had been reactivated and soon became a familiar energy in my life that was now easier to access and focus. Not only was I creating art, but I was boosting my self-esteem around my ability to think and act creatively.

I decided to take art classes in ceramics because I had heard how relaxing pottery could be, and I found, in addition to needing time to create, I also needed some down time from the stress and strain of the hospital environment. I wound up hating throwing pots on a wheel, but I loved hand-building with clay—it was like being a little kid with a whole room of Play-Doh. I found that simply playing with clay further loosened up my creative energies in ways I would never have dreamed possible. Working with clay was pure pleasure.

I still had another important objective to fulfill in my life: to see more of the world. I set out to do exactly that, just as all these other changes—a new husband, a new career, new artistic endeavors—were unfolding around me. Marrying a man from Ireland meant frequent trips "home" to a new country where I had a new family and made many new acquaintances—experiencing Ireland from the inside out. Consequently, I fell in love with Ireland and am always happy to accompany Stephen there whenever possible. It has also been my good fortune that Stephen, too, loves to travel, and we have spent much of our vacation time not only traveling home to Ireland, but visiting other countries as well.

Thus, the gentle push of envying a dying woman's well-spent life showed me that it is important to listen to my dreams and do whatever I can to fulfill them in the time I am given. But that isn't the end of the story. The dying also showed me something else: happiness doesn't come by merely fulfilling our own dreams. Deep happiness, peace, and a profound gratitude for a well-lived life come when we make it part of our life's work to help others fulfill their own goals, dreams, and potentials. A life lived for others is a deeply satisfying life. Yet, it is in listening to and following our own dreams that we are often best able to help others fulfill their own potential.

How Doing What We Love Can Help Others

The pleasure and enjoyment I received from renewing my interest in art and creating something beautiful began manifesting itself in surprising ways in the rest of my life. I helped established a creative arts program that brought arts and crafts opportunities to our bored and bed-bound, long-term hospital patients. I began seeing the value of helping my patients and their families simply enjoy themselves in whatever manner possible, which can be somewhat limited by illness and being stuck in a hospital. Still, I found that there were all kinds of small things that could be done to help my patients and their families enjoy the moment. At one hospital I helped provide such simple pleasures as ice cream pops for bedridden patients and cappuccinos for their loved ones in the waiting rooms. Elsewhere, I made rounds with the humor cart, which brought comedy DVDs to patients' rooms. I also joined the hospital's "Visiting Clown" Committee. I helped initiate some creative programming for our patients in long-term rehabilitation. At several hospitals where I worked, I was fortunate enough to be able to help organize holiday parties or Easter egg hunts for the sick children.

At one hospital I joined a talented staff member who happened to sing in her church's choir, and every year she organized staff to walk through the hospital corridors, singing holiday carols. While we traveled from unit to unit singing, I noticed something very powerful. The patients and their families were touched and grateful for the songs, and often joined in singing with us, but many of the staff members—doctors and nurses, many of whom I knew personally to be hardworking, yet brusque and emotionally distant—were openly crying, tears streaming down their cheeks. It was a moment I will never forget. I began realizing the deep need so many hospital staff have for respite and reconnecting at an emotional and gut level with their "best selves"—the caring, compassionate selves that originally brought them to medicine.

This moment of epiphany eventually led me to leave direct patient care and enter a new career in hospital mission administration, a career that allows, among other things, for the development of retreat, respite, and support activities for hospital staff and medical personnel.

Simply by joining one woman who had decided that one of her own gifts was to gather people at work to sing holiday carols around the hospital, I was led to enter a new line of work. In my new job, I helped dozens and dozens of caregivers provide better care, not only for their patients, but for themselves and their loved ones. I began organizing staff retreats and a "care cart" that brought mini-massages and hot cocoa to tired and stressed staff members on their units. I also helped the medical staff identify their own talents and interests, and implement events or ongoing projects using these talents for their own good, the good of their coworkers and the good of many others, both locally and globally. We had a nurse who opened her home regularly to host fundraising events, one of which provided a life-changing fistula repair operation for a woman in Ethiopia. Another group of nurses made dolls and toys which accompanied medical personnel making Third World medical mission trips for their tiny patients. And another nurse opened her home, a working horse ranch, so that sixty of her coworkers and their families could have a free and relaxing day off with a picnic, horse rides, and hayrides.

While I missed working directly with the sick and dying, I received immense satisfaction knowing that I was helping other caregivers on the "frontlines" of medicine to enjoy respite opportunities and avoid burnout. I was also delighted to see so much good being multiplied, time and again, by one person doing just one good thing that inspired and led many others to do something of similar good. I knew at a gut level that, even though I was no longer working directly with the dying, my patients who had "passed on" would be pleased with the work I was now doing, work that would help many more caregivers give better care to the sick and dying because they themselves were learning the value of self-care.

Just as my professional role and identity as a caregiver changed over the years, my ideas concerning travel also grew and expanded. Having the experience of "going home" to Ireland changed the way I saw "foreigners," since I was now married to one! I also remembered my trip to Haiti many years before, when a Haitian woman named Celine had unwittingly introduced me to the joy and satisfaction of caring for the sick and dying.

What I began to realize more and more was that, unlike my hospice patient, Helen, whose good life going on safaris and guided tours to distant lands had inspired my envy and life change, I was really craving a different sort of travel experience. I wanted to experience different countries and cultures more like their actual citizens did, living day to day with local people and helping them achieve their own goals and dreams for better lives and a better world. I wanted to go abroad and make a difference, however small, in the limited time I had in each country I visited.

I began looking for ways to go overseas as a volunteer serving the local people. I embraced the opportunity to go to Bolivia as a translator and chaplain for a medical team doing cleft-palate surgery in a busy hospital in La Paz. While there was very little I was able to do clinically, I was able to work with the Bolivian nurses and show them what I did as a chaplain, and how the presence of a chaplain could enhance a medical team as well as be a real comfort to patients and families. In the end, several of the nurses asked for "chaplaincy training," which I tried to provide for them in the very limited time at our disposal. More important than any actual training, I believe I empowered them to believe that they could do this sort of work. I also tried to leave them with some simple skills and reading materials to enhance the meager training I was able to give them.

In subsequent years, I was able to travel to Poland and Vietnam. In neither of those places did I provide chaplaincy services; instead I taught

English to high school and college students. My Polish and Vietnamese students were delightful young people full of their own hopes and dreams for the future, many of which required a working knowledge of English. I was happy to have some time working outside of the hospital environment, and equally happy to be helping dozens of young adults prepare to be leaders of their developing nations. I began to see more and more clearly that, while health care is an essential human need and that providing spiritual care to the sick and dying is very important work, any work is important work if it empowers others to lead full lives, especially full lives that will multiply the good in this world.

Living a Life Worthy of Your Time Here on Earth

What are you doing with the rest of your life? Are you on the path to fulfilling what you want to do, or have you somehow strayed from a life of meaning and purpose? Have you wandered away from what you should be doing with your life? Do you even know what it is you should be doing? And if not, are you taking the time to find out?

The dying will teach you every time that life is short and that what we are living today—right now—is not a dress rehearsal. There is no shame in not knowing what we should be doing with our lives, nor is there shame in being out of touch with that which would give us profound satisfaction and purpose. The only shame is if we don't attempt to find these important things while there is still time. Start today to live a life worthy of your time here on Earth. Listening to the wisdom of those who have gone before us is the first step.

Over the years, as I shared time with those at the end of life, I saw many of them gradually detach themselves from this world as they prepared for whatever awaited them after death. Among the first "earthly shackles" many dying people throw off are their attachments to negativity and to anything that is not life-giving. Poor and peripheral relationships, institutions, and beliefs that do not serve them—all of these go out the window, as the dying struggle to hold on to that which will give them hope, peace, and meaning in their final days. I found myself needing to do the same, not only as my caregiver career took more and more of my energies, but as I increasingly realized that anything not life-affirming or energy-renewing wasn't worth my time and effort.

I have encountered many negative people and situations throughout my years but, for the most part, you have not heard about them in these accounts. That is because the negative is not worth our time and effort. The dying taught me that life is short, requiring us to *accentuate the positive*, as the old song goes. In focusing on the positive, you will see goodness and life triumph even in the worst of situations, even when people intentionally set out to hurt us.

I have been privileged to hear many inspiring stories from the dying and their loved ones. People have told me they have enjoyed hearing these stories, so I began writing down some of them to share with others. One reader asked me to share more of my stories, and that is how this book came about. It is my ardent hope for you, dear reader, that your own life will be filled with many good stories. May your life's path be rich in love, adventure, good work, and the satisfaction of making this world a better place. Remember: some of the best guidance you'll ever receive in this life will come from the reflections and observations of those living under the shadow of death, life's greatest teacher. Spend time getting to know the sick and dying and you'll discover your life will be better for it.

ACKNOWLEDGEMENTS

M Y HEARTFELT THANKS go out to the following individuals who helped make this book possible:

- To my husband, Stephen Patrick O'Brien, for his ongoing love, support, and accompaniment while I wrote this book. I treasure Stephen's wisdom, affection, and friendship as we continue our "earthly journey" together, serving and caring for those among us in special need of our time, attention, and prayerful assistance.
- To *Spirituality and Health* magazine, which first published my stories and then suggested I write this book, particularly Brian Lewis, Heather Shaw, Matt Sutherland, Victoria Sutherland, and Gary Klinga. Thank you all for encouraging me to pursue this project.
- To my editor, Betsy Robinson, for her tireless work on my manuscript, as well as her heartfelt support, straightforward advice, and insight regarding my work.
- To my clinical pastoral education supervisors, who taught me how to be a chaplain and especially how to reflect upon and write about my experiences.
- To all my colleagues and associates at the various hospices and hospitals where I worked and trained, including the Human Service Alliance of Winston-Salem, North Carolina; Northwestern Memorial Hospital, Chicago; University of Illinois Medical Center at Chicago; Advocate Christ Hospital of Oak Lawn, Illinois; and St. Anthony's Hospital, St. Petersburg, Florida.
- And last but certainly not least, to all my former patients and their families for giving me their affection, trust, wisdom, and prayers throughout my training and career as a chaplain. Each of you abides in my thoughts and prayers until we meet again.

Sources

Albom, Mitch. *Tuesdays with Morrie.* New York: Random House. 1997.

Byock, Ira. *The Four Things that Matter Most: A Book about Living.* New York: Simon and Schuster. 2004.

Callanan, Maggie and Patricia Kelley. *Final Gifts: Understanding the Special Awareness, Needs and Communication of the Dying.* New York: Poseidon Press. 1992.

Callanan, Maggie. *Final Journeys: A Practical Guide for Bringing Care and Comfort at the End of Life.* New York: Bantam. 2009.

Dossey, Larry. "Healing and the Nonlocal Mind." *Alternative Therapies Magazine,* Vol. 5, November 1999.

Guggenheim, Bill and Judy. *Hello from Heaven: A New Field of Research—After-Death Communication—Confirms that Life and Love are Eternal.* New York: Bantam Books. 1995.

Harris, Trudy. *Glimpses of Heaven: True Stories of Hope and Peace at the End of Life's Journey.* Grand Rapids, Michigan: Baker Publishing Group. 2008.

Kübler-Ross, Elisabeth. *On Death and Dying.* New York: Scribner. 1969.

National Hospice and Palliative Care Organization. "Guidelines for Spiritual Care in Hospice." Alexandria, Virginia: 2000.

Suncoast Hospice. "Spiritual Care: The Hospice of the Florida Suncoast." Clearwater, Florida: 1996.

Teasdale, Wayne. *A Monk in the World: Cultivating a Spiritual Life.* Novato, California: New World Library. 2002.

Warner, Melanie. "Healthcare Savings Could Start in the Cafeteria." *NY Times,* November 29, 2009.

Wooten-Green, Ron. *When the Dying Speak: How to Listen and Learn from Those Facing Death.* Chicago: Loyola Press. 2001.